From the Markets of Tuscany

Giulia Scarpaleggia

From the Markets of Tuscany

A collection of traditional, seasonal recipes

Guido Tommasi Editore

OSTERIA
DEL
VICARIO

SUMMARY

Introduction

Friday is market day in Colle Val d'Elsa, and from the early morning hours, something is different in the air.

Dusty old Jeeps and small runabout commercial vehicles are on the road for the occasion, all making their way towards town from the surrounding countryside and villages.

It's a day for catching up with friends and neighbors, a day when old people sporting hats in every season gather for a chat near Piazza Arnolfo, and grandmothers take advantage of the chance to do some shopping, to pay their weekly visit to the doctor and to stop in at the general store to catch up on the latest news with friends. When school is out for the summer, clusters of Italian teenagers loiter in the market square, one of their few opportunities to meet outside the classroom.

To every generation, the market is the beating heart of the town, pulsing with chitchat, friendly shouting and bargaining, and the aroma of roast chicken, croquettes and porchetta.

When I was little, my grandfather Biagio worked in an office that faced on to the marketplace, a snug space with just enough room for his desk, a bookshelf, and a small chair for me to sit when I'd visit. In summer, my father would take us to the Colle market on his way to work.
We would arrive early, when the stands were still getting set up. I'd bring my summer homework with me and be very, very good. Then at mid-morning my grandfather would close up his office and take me for a short walk, holding my hand in his. Sometimes he would take me to have a second breakfast at the bar, other times to buy roast chicken and croquettes to take home for lunch with my grandmother.

In San Gimignano, on the other hand, where I'd go to spend a few days with my other grandfather, Remigio, aunt Silvana and Margherita, market day was Thursday. We'd walk through the entire town, up and down its streets from Porta San Matteo to Porta San Giovanni to get to the market, while my aunt chattered, stopping to greet friends and acquaintances along the way. Then we'd head back home loaded down with shopping bags, ready to sort out all the produce for the coming days' menus as soon as we walked in the door.

When I took up teaching Tuscan cooking classes, I began to appreciate anew just how extraordinary markets are. Strong human ties are formed here—while giving tips on how to cook eggplants, discussing which fish is best suited for the mixed seafood dish *trabaccolara* or the differences between Tuscan and Sienese pecorino cheese.

Travelling around Tuscany for over a year to visit its weekly, large indoor and smaller organic markets was a learning experience, one that helped me to better know and love this region I call home—my place in the world. While I was lost in small talk with local producers, buying everything from honey and local cheeses to pork fat sausages and fragrant peaches, my husband Tommaso would follow me with camera in hand, capturing what was unique about every market and how each differed in character and changed with the seasons.

A crisis of sorts struck me while writing this book: I had serious doubts about how to organize Tuscany into more or less uniform geographic areas. Had I allowed the centuries-old parochialism and derisive hostilities of this region to influence me, this book would have contained more chapters than an encyclopedia. Putting Pisa and Livorno together seemed impossible, and uniting Garfagnana and Lunigiana in the same chapter equally unthinkable, because in spite of their proximity, these are areas with distinctive characters, landscapes, traditions and products.

Ultimately, I chose to gather all the recipes together and divide them into courses in order to avoid upsetting people' sensibility and fueling the geographical "feuds" that characterize this region.

With this book, I would like to take you on a journey through Tuscany at its most genuine, from market to market and recipe to recipe, and finally to the kitchen, where you will be able to recreate the true flavors of this extraordinary region comprised of coasts, mountains, marshy plains, and hills swathed in grapevines and olive trees. You'll learn about traditional breads, from the essential unsalted Tuscan bread to breads made from chestnut flour or potato. The meat dishes include recipes made from game and offal, while the fish recipes range from coastal specialties like the Livornese fish soup *cacciucco* to the fish and vegetable dish from Orbetello known as *pesce all'isolana*. Each chapter is teeming with vegetables and fruit, which should always be selected in accordance with seasonality and local production guidelines.
And lastly, the desserts, recipes encompassing all the traditional flavors, those rustic cookies and cakes of the past, handed down to me by my grandmother.

I hope you will make good use of this book. Smudge its pages with flour and oil.
Take it with you as you travel through Tuscany to discover its markets and local products.
And bring it to life through your own experiences.

A GUIDE TO TUSCAN CITIES AND THEIR FOOD MARKETS

FLORENCE

My Love Affair with Florence

I came to know Florence around age 25, when I left the security of my family home in Val d'Elsa, and Siena, where I had studied, to venture out into the big city. Perhaps owing to my being a country girl, Florence seemed larger than life to my eyes. I found it enormous, chaotic, and yet I freely admit that I immediately fell for Florence's charms.

More a large town than a true city, Florence is still comprised of individual districts, each with its artisan workshops, local markets, small squares and alleyways, in addition to the areas swarming with tourists. Thanks to friends I met there—and, some years later, to love—I discovered a city that I'd not known prior. And I fell in love with it.

I challenge anyone to resist the allure of Piazzale Michelangelo, or San Miniato al Monte, with all of Florence stretched out before you as the Arno River glistens below, as it does in every season and every moment of the day.

Florence was so many things to me. Wandering its streets with a gelato in hand, or exploring its traditional tripe and lampredotto vendors with all manner of people in line: students, workers and tourists. Florence with its central landmark, the Duomo, its historic cafés and evenings spent along the Arno.

It was Florence's markets, however, that ultimately won me over. Drawn in by the colors and aromas, at first I would follow the trail of scents, of ripe late-spring strawberries or porcini mushrooms from the fall woods. But then I would get to talking with vendors, who were always happy to share their tales and their recipes, their lively eyes behind heaps of fruits and vegetables.

Located just outside the San Lorenzo and Sant'Ambrogio indoor markets—true Florentine institutions—these neighborhood outdoor farmers markets remain the beating heart of this city. Every morning, in every season, they slowly come to life at the break of day, attracting locals to shop for fruit, vegetables, tripe, salted cod, fresh ricotta and more. Then there's the market at Florence's Piazza delle Cure, near the soccer stadium—one of my favorites. At this market I learned how to make minestrone, while listening in as some produce vendors chattered on.

Some of Florence's more noteworthy squares come to life once a month with local organic markets, starting with the Fierucola market in Santissima Annunziata on the first weekend of the month. Each market day highlights a different product: wool, honey, bread, oil. The third Sunday of the month sees the organic market in Piazza Santo Spirito, while come the first Saturday of the month, Piazza della Repubblica plays hosts to its farmers market, with producers coming in from the Florentine countryside to sell vegetables, organic wine, cheese and honey.

Sant'Ambrogio Market

WHERE: Piazza Ghiberti and Piazza Sant'Ambrogio, Florence.

WHEN: Monday to Saturday, 7am to 2pm.

NOT TO MISS: Maria's organic avocados, seasonal vegetables, roast pork loin with pears, and the chicken galantine from the Valdarno Meat Coop.

WHERE TO EAT: Inside the market at Trattoria Da Rocco for tripe, tongue salad, or the "Albertino", a specialty sandwich made with stewed donkey meat from nearby Semel; or at Chef Fabio Picchi's Cibreo and Teatro del Sale restaurants, at the corner of Piazza Ghiberti.

Just outside Florence's city center, the Duomo and Palazzo della Signoria, and very near the Synagogue, La Nazione newspaper offices, Piazza d'Azeglio and the large boulevards, Sant'Ambrogio market offers everything an Italian—or rather, Tuscan—market should.
Compared to the recently restructured, more centrally located San Lorenzo market, popular primarily with tourists, Sant'Ambrogio is a lively marketplace frequented by Florentines.
The outdoor area offers the usual neighborhood market chaos, with fruit and vegetable stands on one side, and clothes and shoes, plants, flowers and household items on the other.

This is where I go, around the back of the market facing Via de' Macci, to visit the foods section, in particular to stop by Maria's counter, featuring local products as well as oranges, lemons, mandarins, and avocados, all from Sicily. Here I buy bitter oranges for marmalade in winter, and the best avocados I've ever tasted in Italy: small, dark and ripe. Among all the vendors at Sant'Ambrogio market, there's one who is also a farmer, Paolo from the Falani farm, whose hands tell of long hours of work in the fields. Large and strong, they are always poised to point out the best radishes for you, to hand you your bag of purchased goods, to take yours in his in friendly greeting.

The commercial vendors offer several specialty items, exotic fruits, and Asian products like fresh tofu. Albertino's counter sells sandwiches, cold cuts, soft ripened cheeses and raw milk. Open since August 2014, Albertino's counter at Sant'Ambrogio enjoys a loyal clientele. And no wonder. You can't take your eyes off him as he slices up some prosciutto for sandwiches. Although leaving the outdoor market stands with their head-turning colors and aromas is always a bit difficult, the indoor market also deserves attention.
At the outdoor market, fruit and vegetables reign, but inside it's all about meat and fish. Here, the fish counter takes up a large portion of the indoor space, with both fresh and frozen fish on offer. The length of an entire wall, the large counter is set up freshly every day, with sea and fishing zone maps on the wall behind together with informative signs on various types of fish. You can almost smell the saltiness of the sea in the air.

Yet the real star of Sant'Ambrogio's indoor market is meat. Osvaldo, the Lanini chickenery and the Valdarno Carni are more than mere meat counters; they're like small theaters running daily performances, the butchers like congenial storytellers.

10X5.00
FINOCCHI
1.30
BROCCOLI

Polleria
Lanini

San Lorenzo Central Market

WHERE: Between Via dell'Ariento, Via Sant'Antonino, Via Panicale and Piazza del Mercato Centrale.

WHEN: The ground floor is open from Monday to Friday, 7am to 3pm and Saturday from 7am to 5pm, excluding summer months. The street food section is open every day from 9am to midnight.

NOT TO MISS: A chat with Luciano Manetti, a Florentine butcher in business for more than 70 years, or the sliced cold cuts at Pierini.

WHERE TO EAT: Take a seat at one of the small tables at Da Nerbone for a sandwich or dish of lampredotto, or try the lampredotto sandwich at Beatrice Trambusti's stall in Via dell'Ariento, just across from the market entrance.

OUTSIDE THE MARKET: A stop at the nearby historic perfumery and herbalist shop Officina Profumo Farmaceutica di Santa Maria Novella to pick up some Alchermes, made according to a recipe developed by the then-director, friar Cosimo Bucelli, in 1743.

Just a few minutes from the Duomo, San Lorenzo Central Market is interesting for its architectural merits, having been designed by Giuseppe Mengoni, the architect responsible for the Vittorio Emanuele II shopping arcade in Milan, who took inspiration from the Halles market in Paris. Glass and iron elements lend this building an imposing look, and the large overhead windows allow natural light to enter and fill up the space.

Today, San Lorenzo market is more popular with tourists than Florentines, given its central location so close to the Duomo. It's worth a visit all the same, not only for its architecture but also for the historical importance it represents, its picturesque stalls and traditional Florentine dishes such as tripe and lampredotto.

A recent restoration has transformed the top floor of the market into an area dedicated to more contemporary concepts, such as street food, together with a cooking school, and vendors of pizza, fresh pasta, meat and fish. Choose what you like to eat and take a seat at one of the stools or the small tables in the center of the space.

The heart of the market, however, is the ground floor, with its butchers, fruit and vegetable vendors, deli and tripe counters, bakers and fishmongers—all set up in their specific areas based on the natural ventilation of the building. Here you'll also find offal, a favorite among Florentines, from cheek and stomach and lungs to testicles, tails, paws, tripe, tendons, udders and *ventricino*, cured pork fat encased in stomach lining or intestine. Next to the fruit, vegetables, fish and meat areas is Pierini's counter, a popular lunch spot among Florentines. One look at the counter is enough to appreciate the wide selection of cold cuts, prosciutto, salamis and cheeses. Most of the products on offer here are Tuscan, coming from small farms and butchers. For a while now they've been offering hot dishes like pappa al pomodoro and ribollita, in addition to the nearly 40 types of sauces on display for pasta and crostini, all made with pride by the proprietors.

Santo Spirito in Oltrarno, Florence's market south of the river

WHERE: Piazza Santo Spirito, Florence.

WHEN: The third Sunday of every month, excluding August.

NOT TO MISS: The ricotta necci made by the Andreotti family, the herbs grown at La Penta farm, the raw honey and extracts made by Gigliola and Giovanni, the basil pesto from Roberta together with Antico Colle Fiorito's Tuscan pecorino cheese.

WHERE TO EAT: Sabatino, a traditional and unpretentious Florentine trattoria in the San Frediano district, or La Casalinga in Santo Spirito. For a lovely gelato, head to Piazza Tasso and find La Sorbettiera.

Florence is divided into districts, each with its own distinct and recognizable feel. Whereas the areas most known to tourists are those around the Duomo and Piazza della Signoria, crossing the Arno river takes you to the quieter and more authentic area of Florence known as the Oltrarno, and its districts San Frediano and Santo Spirito. Here you still find artisan workshops and locals who greet each other on the street. Everyone knows each other, and locals here feel they come from a separate town within the city of Florence.

In Piazza Santo Spirito, otherwise known simply as Santo Spirito, every third Sunday sees the farmers market, offering organic and biodynamic products.

The scene is rowdy, lively, spontaneous. Here everyone is a farmer or producer, bringing the very best of their seasonal crops. They've all known each other for years and lend each other a hand when needed. Everyone brings along something they've made to share come lunch, eaten together at a long table.

Imagine the perfect farmers market. Santo Spirito's is not far off the idea you've formed in your head. Here you'll find stone ground flours, honey, organic fruit and vegetables, bread and sweets made with marmalade, preserves from Antico Colle Fiorito, cheeses, organic wines, and even plants to start up your own garden.

A special mention must go to the necci (crêpes made with chestnut flour) made by the Andreotti family of the farm L'Alberaccio, for 30 years a regular fixture at the Fierucola market in Piazza Santissima Annunziata. Today they sell their necci in Santo Spirito as well. They farm their own estate of about 10 hectares, including a wooded area. A small part of their enterprise is growing garden vegetables, apples and pears. But chestnuts make up most of their production.

The chestnuts are dried in the traditional way, then ground at a certified stone mill. With the resulting flour, they make necci with ricotta. Stop by to chat with them, and observe what attention they pay to preparing their snack.

CHIANTI AND VAL D'ELSA

Home. The Val d'Elsa and Chianti

I have so many memories of my hometown: My first trip to the market with friends, the first time going to the movies without grown-ups, the first time I bought a Mickey Mouse comic book with my allowance, taking the bus home and feeling so independent, and all my experiences on up through high school...

Today I live just a few kilometers from Colle, in the country house where my father and grandmother were born. I go to the Colle market almost every week, often accompanying tourists enrolled in my cooking classes. Val d'Elsa is nestled right in the heart of Tuscany, halfway between the provinces of Florence and Siena, traversed by the ancient pilgrim route Via Francigena that once wound through the hills left of the Elsa river. Unknown to many and certainly less popular with tourists than Monteriggioni and San Gimignano, Val d'Elsa is dearer to me, with its lovely farmed countryside between Casole and Sovicille, the woods close to my home and the vine- and olive tree-covered hills around Certaldo.

Not far from here is one of Tuscany's most popular regions, Chianti. Who hasn't heard of Chianti at least once? Although known throughout the world for its foremost product, Chianti has so much more than wine to offer tourists and weekend explorers. Driving through Castellina, Greve, Panzano, Radda, Gaiole and Castelnuovo Berardenga, what strikes you first are the soft, rolling hills, the orderly vineyards and the shimmery silver landscape of olive groves. Here and there you spot a quaint village, church or castle, farmhouses, clusters of isolated homes...

The cooking of Val d'Elsa and Chianti are very similar, and each wholly reflects its location between Siena and Florence. Olive oil, unsalted bread, cured meats, eggs, small farm animals, cheese, fruit and vegetables are but some of the fundamental components of our cuisine. This is the land of my grandmother and her recipes, the cuisine I was raised on and later fell so in love with became my passion and my profession.

Every town in the region has its market day, once weekly or more frequently. Tuesday is market day in Poggibonsi, in Certaldo it's on Wednesday, in San Gimignano it's on Thursday and in Colle Val d'Elsa it's Friday. Growing up here, you learn the market location almost like a nursery rhyme. They help you to get your bearings and understand how a usually quiet town can suddenly transform into a lively meeting place, one that draws all who live in the surrounding countryside.

The farmers markets in Val d'Elsa and in the Chianti, on the other hand, take place once a month. At first considered something of a local curiosity, these markets are now quite a routine, like a regular "date" with quality area products. The markets rotate among the towns of Sovicille, Monteriggioni, Poggibonsi and Colle Val d'Elsa, the most interesting among them being that in Greve in Chianti, the Pagliaio farmers market.

Colle Val d'Elsa

WHERE: Piazza Arnolfo, Piazza Sant'Agostino, and adjacent roads, Colle Val d'Elsa.

WHEN: Fridays, 8am to 1:30pm.

NOT TO MISS: Andrea and Jessica's fruit and vegetable stand.

WHERE TO EAT: Bel Mi'Colle trattoria on Via Garibaldi for authentic, simple Tuscan dishes.

OUTSIDE THE MARKET: Grab a gelato from Gelateria Buekke a Gracciano on Via Fratelli Bandiera 81. Try the pine nut gelato, without a doubt my favorite.

Before dawn on Fridays, Colle is an average provincial town, sleepy and quiet. As soon as the sun rises, however, all that changes. Vendors invade Piazza Arnolfo, the main piazza in the modern part of town known as Colle Bassa (lower Colle), while traffic officers have their hands full directing the arriving vehicles. Slowly the piazza and surrounding streets begin to fill up, from the Teatro del Popolo theater—a source of great pride to locals—to Piazza Sant'Agostino.

Come Friday, the market works its magic on everyone: young and old, town-dwellers and countryside residents. They all meet in the piazza for a chat, to visit the doctor's office, to do the shopping, or merely to see friends and catch up on the latest news—births, deaths, weddings.

Colle's market is your classic weekly Italian market, offering just about everything, from shoes, clothing and purses to tablecloths and other household items. The food stands are located at opposite sides of the market. Across from the Teatro del Popolo are those selling cheese, porchetta and candy. The fish counter, managed by two young adults who always have the freshest catch (mostly from the Tyrrhenian Sea), is a perfect addition to this Friday market. Cooking tips come along with your purchase, as well as a friendly dose of teasing: "Ignore the sole! Try the mullet or mackerel instead."

The rotisserie counters with their spitfire chickens and other roasted foods emit the unmistakable aroma of Sunday. No matter the time of day, there's always a line out front, everyone eager to pick up some roasted chicken and potato croquettes.

On the other side of the market are the fruit and vegetable stands, cheese counters and vendors selling traditional products from Sicily and Campania. Really, how can one resist a just-delivered buffalo milk mozzarella? I spend a lot of time here among the fruit and veg, where I often stop with students taking my classes. Sometimes I break to chat with Andrea and Jessica, who only recently opened their stand yet have quickly become regular fixtures here in Colle.

Many of the Colle vendors travel to other area markets in Val d'Elsa, so wherever you go to shop—whether Poggibonsi or Certaldo or one of the small neighborhood markets in Gracciano and Casole—familiar smiles always await you.

Certaldo

WHERE: Viale Giacomo Matteotti, Certaldo.

WHEN: Wednesdays, from 8am to 1pm.

NOT TO MISS: Erica's Certaldo onions.

WHERE TO EAT: Osteria La Saletta, at via Roma 4. In the lower part of town, the typical Tuscan osteria where locals go to taste Giampiero's dishes. Super recommended is the truffle risotto and Chianti tuna.

OUTSIDE THE MARKET: Every year in July, Certaldo hosts the international street theater festival, Mercantia. On these midsummer evenings, the squares and streets of the medieval village fill up with theatrical companies, street artists, contemporary art, artisans and good food.

Certaldo is a medieval hamlet in the Val d'Elsa area. Its fortunate position along the Via Francigena and near Florence has always meant much traffic and exchange here. Surrounded by rolling hills swathed in olive groves and vineyards, this lively town hosts regular summer food and wine events and popular festivals.

When I was in high school, I thought of Certaldo as the birthplace of medieval writer Boccaccio, author of *The Decameron,* considered one of the cornerstones of Italian literature alongside Dante and Petrarch.

The 100 novellas that comprise *The Decameron* speak to the joy of being alive, with tales of escaping death and the blending of the pleasures of the table with the pleasures of the flesh in uninhibited and ironic tales. From the story of Chichibìo and the crane, to Ciacco and Biondello's pranks at the Argenti lunch and Bengodi's town with its mountain of Parmigiano cheese, the role of food in *The Decameron* intrigued me back then and had me preferring Boccaccio's novellas to Petrarch's sonnets.

Certaldo's weekly Wednesday morning market is a great time to meet producers, to watch the lively comings and goings of locals, visit stalls and browse merchandise. Area specialty products include wine, olive oil, Tuscan white truffles and the Certaldo red onion, a Slow Food presidium. When in season, Certaldo onions color the fruit and vegetable stands an intense red. They are a source of great pride to locals.

The custom here is for the deli vans to mix in with the fish, cheese and vegetable stands, which then gradually give way to the clothing and shoes stalls. While browsing this market, the various aromas blend and fill your head with ideas and pairings.

Certaldo, as you may have heard, is a burgh of Val d'Elsa situated in our country, which, small though it be, was once inhabited by gentlemen and men of substance...

Giovanni Boccaccio, *The Decameron*

CIPOLLA
DI
CERTALDO

Aromi del Chianti
dal 1984
coltivazione locale
Zafferano
Zafferano
Tregole
Erbe da Cucina
Duccio Fontani
Tregole
Castellina in Chianti
FONTANI DUCCIO
Krauter
aus eigenem Anbau
Épices
de mes champs
Spices
grown on my fields

Greve in Chianti

WHERE: Piazza Matteotti, Greve in Chianti.

WHEN: Every fourth Sunday of the month, until the afternoon.

NOT TO MISS: Kirstie's ceramic wares, the soft caprino goat cheese from the small Podere Le Fornaci farm, the wicker and reed items (and tales!) from Giocondo Fagioli.

WHERE TO EAT: Have a platter of cured meats or the steak tartare at Antica Macelleria Falorni, or a salad or local specialty dish at Osteria Mangiando Mangiando, both located in Piazza Matteotti.

OUTSIDE THE MARKET: Pay a visit to Podere Le Fornaci, a few kilometers from the market, to see how they make their excellent cheeses.

Greve is not far from me, located right in the heart of the Chianti area, a little less than an hour from both Florence and Siena. It makes for a great day trip from either of these cities, especially in spring or fall. With its wine, numerous cellars open to the public, and picture-postcard landscape of olive groves, vineyards, rolling hills, small churches and farmhouses, Greve is a lovely destination for shopping for local products.

Every fourth Sunday of the month, Greve also hosts an organic foods and antiques market called Il Pagliaio in Piazza Matteotti, the center of town just near the Falorni butchery.

More than 40 farmers attend this market, bringing everything from fruit, vegetables, bread and sweets to woven flower garlands, plants, wooden cutting boards, ceramics, saffron, herbs, soaps, wine and olive oil. Each month the market chooses a theme and organizes workshops, meetings and demonstrations. When the market dedicated to wool was on, for example, yarns and antique spinning wheels were on display to admire. There was even a knitting workshop.

Depending on the season, you'll find everything from wild berries and plumps, juicy tomatoes to local honeys, breads and focaccia made from heritage grains, pretty chestnuts from the Casentino or Mugello regions, loquats and quinces, and onions in their shiny red and purple coats. Everything is fresh, vibrant, ready to be transformed into something good.

The stands and counters at this market vary from time to time, yet some are regulars, such as farmer Duccio Fontani from Tregole in the Chianti, who grows aromatic and medicinal herbs on a small scale. Here you'll find saffron, dried herb blends for meat roasts, salads and cheeses, and aromatic herbs for cooking. He speaks several languages and will catch and hold your attention with his eccentric, congenial nature.

This is a market unique in its kind. All the products are local, fresh, organic, hand made, or grown by the attending farmers, with whom you can chat and exchange tips, suggestions and interesting recipes.

SIENA AND VAL D'ORCIA
A Natural and Cultural Treasure

I spent my university years in Siena, a medieval town with strong ties to the surrounding Tuscan countryside. In winter, fierce winds blow through the narrow streets and piazza, glimpses of which come upon you like a sudden and unexpected picture postcard. I grew up here and am used to the beauty of this place. Tourists, though, those who come to this part of Tuscany to take my cooking classes, for instance, are always stunned by Siena's enchanting medieval atmosphere, its merchants, bankers, and spice shops.

A predominantly relaxed feel reigns in Siena for most of the year, yet come July and August with the arrival of the Palio, everything changes. The town bursts into life with vibrant colors, flags and much enthusiastic shouting during this historic, thrilling horse race.

South of Siena the landscape changes, gradually giving way to gently rolling hills that capture the imagination year round, from the first tender green shoots in springtime to the color-laden mists of late fall.
This remarkable area was granted UNESCO World Heritage Site status in 2004.

The valley through which the Orcia river peacefully runs was entirely redrawn when it was annexed by Siena between the 14th and 15th centuries, shaped by Renaissance ideals of good government, and resulting in aesthetically pleasing landscapes. The Val d'Orcia has long inspired artists with its natural beauty, farms, hilltop fortress towns and villages, bridges, abbeys and the Via Francigena that passes through.

Today it is famous for its cypress trees, those fine lines of deep green that seem drawn with an ink pen, along with the traditional pici pasta, renowned cheeses like Pecorino di Pienza and its celebrated wine, Brunello di Montalcino.

A good time to visit the Val d'Orcia is from April to October, when the weather is fine or at least milder than wintertime, when finding accommodation, open restaurants or artisan shops can be a challenge. Visiting in the off season, however, offers a great deal more to those interested in a nature experience over a touristic one, who love the feel of a sleepy town in late November or the joys of solitude while driving from town to town through the valleys. The Val d'Orcia is truly an open-air treasure just waiting to be discovered.

Between Val d'Orcia and the Crete Senesi area is Chianciano, one of Italy's most famous thermal spa regions, known as far back as the Etruscan and Roman eras.

Around here, the weekly markets alternate their local producers. They often take place on the weekend, giving visitors the perfect excuse to tour the area's medieval towns in any season, while enjoying breathtaking views.

The Farmers Market in Siena

WHERE: La Lizza, Siena.

WHEN: Fridays, from 8am to 1pm.

NOT TO MISS: The wine and spelt flour from Il Ciliegio farm, the herbs and selection of chili from around the world at Vivaio delle Volte nursery.

WHERE TO EAT: At Gino Cacino in Piazza del Mercato for a lunch of excellent cheeses, homemade mustards and jams, and grilled bread with unusual and decadent toppings.
Or at Osteria La sosta di Violante on Via Pantaneto for a traditional Tuscan meal with a unique twist.

OUTSIDE THE MARKET: Coffee roasters Caffè Fiorella on Via di Città is one of the best cafes in Siena, offering pastries equally good.

Wednesday has always been market day in Siena. When I was at university, I had to remember to leave earlier on market day to beat the traffic, as finding a parking spot around the fortress, the heart of the marketplace, was nearly impossible. A great deal of movement and excitement always marked mid-week, with everyone eager to join in the area's largest and most vibrant market.

Considering its variety, the food section at this market is really rather small, but it is well stocked with fruit and vegetables, a few fresh fish counters and the obligatory rotisserie counter filling the entire market with aromas of roasted chicken and fried polenta.

Recently, a Friday morning farmers market has started up at La Lizza, just along the tree-lined boulevard that runs from the fortress into town.
The seasonal fruit and vegetables catch your eye immediately with their rustic freshness—and the occasional dirt clump, remnant of the veggie patch.

The nearby Il Ciliegio farm in Monteriggioni sells wheat, chickpea and spelt flours, fragrant breads and their own wines. The Vivaio delle Volte nursery has what is perhaps the showiest stand, displaying countless varieties of chili peppers from around the world along with herbs, including the rare and almost legendary Sienese dragoncello, or tarragon.

The girls from Podere Le Lapole farm offer an incredible selection of sourdough baked products made with their own flours, including multi-grain, rosemary, sweet breads with figs and of course Tuscan bread, cookies, breadsticks and focaccia breads made with corn and onion. Stop by and choose a fragrant loaf and some cookies for a quick snack.

Naturally this farmers market also has meats on offer, as well as pecorino cheeses and organic pasta from Le Casacce, who also sell heritage, stone-ground grain, spelt and barley flours and jams.

Aromatiche
€ 2.50
Melissa
Menta
Basilico

LIBERAMENTE OSTERIA
BAR

The Christmas Market in Siena

WHERE: Piazza del Campo, Siena.

WHEN: One of the first weekends in December.

NOT TO MISS: The Cinta Senese cured meats from Spannocchia Farm.

OUTSIDE THE MARKET: Founded in 1879, Antica Drogheria Manganelli on Via di Città makes Sienese *panforte* according to an ancient recipe. Here you will find all the spices needed to make *panforte* at home, together with ingredients used in many other traditional Sienese desserts.

In summertime, come Saturday nights we used to sit down in Piazza del Campo with a gelato. I could feel the warmth from the sun-baked bricks below me. It was like being at the center of the world, with those historic palaces lit up from all sides and the contrada flags flying during the Palio horse race.
In those moments I felt this piazza could not have been lovelier. But I was wrong.

For some years now, Piazza del Campo has seen the revival of its grand historic weekly market, with roots in the 13th century.

During one of the first weekends in December, the square fills up with stands decorated with flickering lights and creating a mercantile feel of days long gone. This is one of the loveliest Christmas markets around, featuring traditional agricultural products and locally crafted artisan goods.

Each vendor tries to tempt you to taste their wares, like a scene straight out of an imaginary medieval market. The large wheels of Pienza pecorino and Sienese pecorino cheeses on display brighten the scene with various shades of brown-, ochre- and red-colored rinds. Strung sausage links hang above the heads of vendors, who in the meantime are busy slicing their cured prosciutto by hand.

The smell of cured meats competes with the aroma of spices from the panforte, panpepato, cavallucci and ricciarelli. The unrivaled stars of this market, traditional Sienese Christmas desserts, are rooted in the apothecary workshops and the homes of wealthy merchants here in the Middle Ages.

Pienza

WHERE: Piazza Galletti, Pienza.

WHEN: Every first Sunday of the month, all day.

NOT TO MISS: The organic raw milk pecorino cheese from Podere Il Casale farm and the Cinta Senese cured meats from Mario Vigni's farm.

WHERE TO EAT: At Bandita Townhouse on Corso il Rossellino, 111, a welcoming, modern eatery popular with locals. For a quick snack head to Osteria Sette di Vino in Piazza di Spagna, where owner Luciano will speak to you in any of the 15 different languages on their menu.

OUTSIDE THE MARKET: Pay a visit to Podere Il Casale for their cheeses and shop at the small Cacio di Ernello. Visit the Ferro Battuto Biagiotti show room, makers of hand-crafted wrought iron items (with a shop in Pienza and a workshop just outside town). Next is Aracne for scarves, stoles, tablecloths, blankets and curtains, handmade right in the shop from entirely natural yarns and fabrics. Keep your eyes open for the lovely Pienza fabric, with its intricate diamond-shaped design.

Pienza was once a village in decline. It was known as Corsignano until 1462 when Enea Silvio Piccolomini, born there 53 years prior, was elected pope and took the name Pius II. Once made pope, Pius II enlisted an important architect of the time, Bernardo Rossellino, to redesign his village. Rossellino did this and more: he changed Pienza's fate by constructing an entirely new town inspired by Renaissance esthetics. He named the town Pienza in honor of Pope Pius. Today Pienza is a tranquil hilltop town that still maintains this romantic Renaissance look. Park outside the town center and walk along the narrow streets, seeking out enchanting alleyways like Via del Bacio, Via dell'Amore and Via della Fortuna. Then take in the ancient walls and the views of the Val d'Orcia that stretch out before you.

Every first Sunday of the month, the organic market in Pienza's Piazza Galletti—a small square with fishbone design brick pavement—offers traditional products from the Val d'Orcia estate. Area producers line their stands up one next to the other to display their organic, highest quality wines, olive oils, breads and grains, but above all the celebrated cheese, Pecorino di Pienza. Pienza pecorino has ancient origins, as attested to by Pliny the Elder's mention of sheep breeding farms in Tuscany in Roman times. Yet further evidence suggests sheep farms were present in this area even earlier, as far back as the Etruscan era. This cheese, said to have been a favorite of Lorenzo de' Medici's, is made with raw whole milk from partially free range sheep raised exclusively on local feeds. The Val d'Orcia, though incredibly beautiful, is a challenging land to cultivate, given its high clay levels and nutrient-poor soil. What does grow here are wormwood, meadow goat's beard, juniper, bird's foot trefoil and salad burnet. The sheep of this region feed on these plants, accounting for Pienza pecorino's unique aroma.

The cheese is coagulated using both calf rennet and artichoke rennet, the latter an ancient vegetable rennet made from the stamens of area wild artichokes. This unique production results in a cheese that is chalky, not stringy, and fabulous when soft, aged slightly or medium aged. It goes well with fava beans and is wonderful for cooking. Once you've visited the market, head to Buon Gusto for an all natural gelato made with seasonal ingredients. Depending on the season, try the strawberry and rosemary flavor or the white coffee, made by infusing coffee beans overnight.

PECORINO DI

AREZZO, VAL D'ARNO AND VAL DI CHIANA

The Arno Valley lies in the easternmost part of Tuscany, encompassing the Arezzo area and bordered by the upper Tiber Valley, the Apennine mountains and the wooded Casentino mountains. This fertile land is home to the Val di Chiana, known for its "white giants" of Tuscany, the Chianina cattle breed. It is a peaceful farming region that also produces the majority of Tuscany's fruit, mostly pears and apples.
In his 1817 work *Italian Journey*, the German writer Goethe expressed his admiration for the Val di Chiana and its thriving agriculture, having observed Arezzo and the extraordinary surrounding plains.

> *You'd be hard pressed to find a more orderly countryside: not a single patch of green is out of place, and everything is as tidy as can be. Wheat grows very well here, given the favorable natural conditions. Following the wheat harvest, broad beans will be planted, to be turned into horse feed along with oats. Lupin beans are also grown here, and will turn a magnificent green before being ready for harvest in March. As well as flax, a cold-resistant crop made even hardier by frost.*
>
> Johann Wolfgang Goethe, *Italian Journey* (1786-1788)

Arezzo and its environs have given the world many noted artists, such as Michelangelo, Petrarch, Masaccio and Piero della Francesca. It was also one of the first episcopal seats in Tuscany, which was to have no small influence on its wealth and subsequently its refined, French-influenced cuisine, as evidenced by its most famous dessert, *il gattò* (*gâteau* in French).

Another star of traditional local cuisine is meat, and not only Chianina beef but also the celebrated Valdarno chicken breed, game meats and, last but not least, pork, in particular porchetta.

Slow Food held its first "Mercato della Terra" in Montevarchi in the Valdarno, a reflection of the area emphasis on locally grown foods and food chain quality. Along with the now historic covered market in Montevarchi, various weekly markets take place throughout the region.

The English musician Sting keeps a home in Valdarno, at Villa del Palagio not far from Figline, where he grows fruit and vegetables and produces cured meats, olive oil, wine and honey.

Arezzo

WHERE: Under the Via Roma portico and near Piazzetta Sopra i Ponti in Arezzo.

WHEN: The first Saturday of the month, from 9am to 7pm.

NOT TO MISS: The goat's milk liqueur made by the kids from Extravaganti and the traditional cold cuts at La Bottega del Sambudello.

WHERE TO EAT: At La Formaggeria located at Via de' Redi 16 to taste not only a vast and detailed selection of cheeses but also traditional dishes such as tripe and Chianina beef tartare.

OUTSIDE THE MARKET: Vestri, one of the Tuscany's top craft chocolate makers, has been producing excellent chocolate in Arezzo for over 30 years. You'll find their chocolate bars, chocolate creams and ancient recipes at the shop located at Via Romana 161 b/c.

When I was ten years old, my uncles took me along with them to Arezzo, where they could indulge their passion for antiques markets. It was the beginning of summer. I'm sure I was a little grouchy that day, utterly oblivious to the charms of the antiques fair, seeing as the shoes I was wearing were too tight. I remember how happy I was that evening, though, when we sat down to have a pizza with prosciutto just outside Arezzo, and I was finally able to rest my feet, fill my belly and leave the hot day behind me. It took returning to Arezzo at an older age to truly comprehend all I had missed that day.

The Arezzo antiques fair started in 1968 and since then has been drawing some 20,000 visitors from around the world every first weekend of the month. A visit to this fair is not unlike traipsing through a huge attic full of treasures, only outside among historic palaces, frescoed churches, alleyways and loggias. A bit of everything is on offer here, from enamel plates and precious fabrics to old dressers and vintage postcards.

On Saturday, alongside the various rare antiques there's also Campagna Aperta ("Open Country"), a market made possible by the Italian environmentalist group Legambiente, held under the Via Roma porticoes near Piazzetta Sopra i Ponti.

Say hello to the young people from Extravaganti, who raise donkeys on the Alpe della Luna nature reserve in San Sepolcro and make unique donkey milk products, including soaps, fragrant elderberry syrup and a milky-white, fresh-tasting liqueur.

The true stars under this portico, however, are the cured meats made from the Cinta Senese pig breed, the cow's and sheep's milk cheeses, oranges, mandarins and vegetables. And of course Val di Chiana apples, available in every kind and color, all grown within a short distance. Don't miss the honeys, truffles, wine and vinsanto, extra virgin olive oil and jams. Naturally you will want to try some of Arezzo's artisanal chocolate, too.

La Bottega

ARMACIA

Montevarchi, the First Earth Market

WHERE: Piazzale dell'Antica Gora 6, Montevarchi.

WHEN: Monday to Saturday, 9am to 1pm and 4pm to 8:30pm.

NOT TO MISS: The Zolfini beans sold in bulk, the Valdarno chicken, soft cheeses and local cured meats.

WHERE TO EAT: Menchetti dal 1948 for breads and pizza made with Verna heritage wheat, located at Via Cassia 9 in Marciano della Chiana, Arezzo.

OUTSIDE THE MARKET: Be sure to try the Valdarno specialty cured meat product *la tarese* at either Mauro Cioni butchery shop or Marco Fantechi's shop, both in Montevarchi.

Montevarchi hosted the first Slow Food market, a project known as Mercato della Terra ("Earth Market") that has since spread throughout Italy and the world.
Inaugurated on February 2, 2008, today it is a direct sales point for numerous local producers.
Following the Slow Food philosophy of "good, clean and fair," this market also brings together area farmers and consumers, who can purchase quality local and seasonal foods directly from those who produce them.

This market offers almost exclusively certified products recognized with the geographical indication labels DOP, IGP, DOCG, DOC and IGT, all from organic or integrated farms.

Quality and commitment to transparency are reflected in every item on offer here, values easily discernible with just a quick look around. Strict adherence to seasonality and the beautiful diversity of nature are also evident, in everything from olive oil, wine and cheeses to the famous Valdarno chickens, farm fresh eggs, spelt flour pasta, and local legume varieties such as zolfini beans from Casentino.

You'll also find schiacciata and daily fresh bread (or day-old bread, good for making soups and salads).
An entire wall of neatly ordered jars holds even more products, like apple juice, honey, jams, mostarda (preserved fruits), and products made with local truffles and the purest saffron.

For variety and selection, it's not unlike a supermarket, only that here every product's origins are traceable, and the farms, producers and faces of the locals behind them all guarantee uppermost quality of everything that ends up on its shelves.

LUNIGIANA

I came to know Lunigiana at the start of a very hot summer.
This slice of Tuscany wedged between Liguria and the sea, the Apuane Alps and Emilia Romagna exhibits interesting influences of its surrounding territories, discernible in Lunigiana accents as well as its cuisine—a cuisine strongly linked to the forest. Chestnuts and mushrooms, for instance, have fed the peasants from Lunigiana for generations.

Driving through this region is an unusual experience, especially for those accustomed to the rolling hills, vineyards and olive groves of Chianti. This is a different Tuscany altogether, unexpected, full of chestnut woods, castles and watermills, and cascading brooks that widen and subside as they reach the lower foothills. Lunigiana is also a mysterious land, replete with tales of haunted castles and legends about the werewolf of *Pontremoli* and *buffardelli*, mischievous sprites who inhabit the woods of northern Tuscany. Equally intriguing are Lunigiana's origins, said to be linked to Luni, a Roman city razed during the barbarian invasions from which the region takes its name.

This is a poor land, yet one that has managed to develop and transform local production into its crowning achievement: chestnut flour, honey, olive oil, Bigliolo beans, *rotelle* apples, barley, spelt, and cheeses made from sheep, cow and goat milk. Lunigiana is also home to two Slow Food presidia, the bread known as *pane marocca di Casola* and the *Zerasca di Zeri* lamb breed.

The sparseness and humble standing of this place together with a sense of being in a "lesser" Tuscany mean that Lunigiana is a land open to discovery, a place eager to tell its story and lure visitors to an atypical holiday in agritourism structures tucked away deep in the natural wilderness. In Lunigiana, this is a wilderness tamed only by the ongoing labor and doggedness of humankind.

Visiting the farms, cheese producers and mills is the best way to discover all that is good and authentic in Lunigiana. It's an ideal destination not only for gourmets and food lovers but also those who love outdoor activities such as biking, horseback riding, and canyoneering. Other possibilities include touring the marble producing area of Carrara and walking the history-rich Via Francigena, which enters the Tuscan region here.
Today Lunigiana's markets continue to represent the rich variety of markets in Tuscany. In remote villages scattered throughout the hills, weekly markets remain an important event for the local residents, while farmers markets offer locally produced items like cheese and cured meats (given the influence of nearby Emilia Romagna). A strong bread culture also thrives here; types differ from town to town and are a source of both great pride and competitive spirit. In three different towns along the Via del Pane or "Bread Road," you'll find three different breads: the bread made in Vinca, that from Agnino and that of Uglianfreddo.
Fivizzano, moreover, is home to Sapori, a three-day street market and medieval fair that brings together farmers and peasants, artisans and storytellers.

GAS

Fivizzano

WHERE: On the streets of Fivizzano.

WHEN: Usually the first weekend of June.

NOT TO MISS: The China (a kind of bitters) from Farmacia Clementi, the cow's milk cheeses from Azienda Agricola Cormezzano and all the local products at Agribottega del Gusto.

WHERE TO EAT: During the Fivizzano Sapori fair there are food stands along the town streets where you can try traditional local dishes cooked by area women.

Giosuè Carducci described Fivizzano as a pearl lost among the mountains. Despite its distance from Florence and its remote mountain location, Fivizzano was the seat of a captaincy of the Florentine Republic in the 15th and 16th centuries, which accounts for the town's Medici style urban plan.

Until last century it was considered "the Florence of Lunigiana." In the 1800s it was home to 80 university graduates, a literary academic and a Medici-style piazza with a beautiful late 17th-century Baroque fountain. Numerous figures in literature and music have lived here.

Today Fivizzano remains a fascinating place, yet is still affected by its isolated location. During the first weekend of June, however, the town undergoes a transformation. For more than 20 years, the streets of this Medici hamlet have been hosting Fivizzano Sapori, a trade fair featuring food and wine specialties of the Massa Carrara province and neighboring areas.

Along the town streets you'll find breads like *panigacci* and the region's most famous bread, *marocca di Casola, testaroli* (a thick pasta usually cut into triangle shapes), the sweet and slightly sour local apples known as *rotelle*, Lunigiana honey DOP, cured meats, cow and goat milk cheeses, *pattona di Agnino* (a chestnut flour cake similar to *castagnaccio*), Treschietto onions, chestnut flour, Garfagnana *necci*, and DOC and IGT wines from Colli di Candia and Val di Magra. You can also taste savory quiches made from wild greens or leek and potato, potato bread and local craft beers.

Women of the area meet in a communal kitchen in the town center to prepare traditional recipes for locals and visitors, who will enjoy them outside under a pergola. In a large pot, the women stir an enormous quantity of polenta cooked in pork bone broth with borlotti beans, potatoes and kale. The polenta is served with cheese and olive oil, or thinly sliced then fried. The smells emitted by that communal kitchen waft through all the town streets, immediately grabbing your attention and stirring your appetite.

Then the streets fill up with storytellers, theatrical characters acting out tales and legends, musicians and ladies performing courtly dances, flag throwers and bands.

Pontremoli

WHERE: Piazza della Repubblica, Pontremoli.

WHEN: Wednesday mornings.

NOT TO MISS: The apples and walnuts from Il Quadrifoglio farm.

WHERE TO HAVE BREAKFAST: You mustn't miss a coffee accompanied by an *amor* pastry at l'Antica Pasticceria degli Svizzeri in Piazza della Repubblica.

OUTSIDE THE MARKET: Check the association Farfalle in Cammino for activities throughout the Lunigiana area like walking, cycling, food and wine excursions.

Pontremoli is a beautiful, history-rich town overlooked by Piagnaro Castle. A diverse food and wine scene thrives here, giving us such specialties as *testaroli*, wild greens savory quiche, the *amor* pastries and the cake known as *la spongata*.

In Pontremoli's Piazza della Repubblica you'll find Antica Pasticceria degli Svizzeri, a pastry shop with a long history. During the Napoleonic era, many Swiss families left the Canton of Grisons and came to Italy to open craft businesses. During this era, the Aitcha family founded their pastry and coffee shop here in Pontremoli, where for six generations they have been serving *amor*—delicate, square-shaped pastries made according to their secret recipe. With the first taste of *amor*, their double layer of fine wafers and rich chantilly cream filling, you will immediately get what all the fuss is about.

Another traditional dessert of the Pontremoli area is the cake *la spongata*, known in Sarzana as spungata and likely Jewish in origin. The recipe for *spongata* arrived in Italy in the 16th century, brought by Sephardic Jews fleeing the Spanish Inquisition. The base ingredients include dried and candied fruits, similar to charoset, a very sweet paste made with dried fruit (not unlike a dense jam) prepared for Pesach (Jewish Easter). Its name derives from the traditional Spanish dessert *lo spongado* but is also related to *spongato*, the spongy sugar once packaged in large cubes for transport. Spongata cake is, in fact, covered in a characteristic sugar glaze that preserves it for a long time.

The Pontremoli market takes place on Wednesdays in the historic town center and hosts numerous clothing, flowers, fruit and vegetable stands, along with rotisseries and local producers who bring along all they've been able to grow, slowly and steadily, throughout the season.

GARFAGNANA

At the start of the 16th century, Ludovico Ariosto, governor of Castelnuovo in Garfagnana under Duke Alfonso d'Este, described the area to his lord as a place where "[...] neither in the woods, nor in the ground, nor locked inside the home is one safe here from murderers and assassins."
Ariosto wasn't terribly fond of this wild, untameable land, inhabited as it was by a fierce people and subject to constant raids by bandits hiding in the mountains.

Garfagnana was for a long time a poor and isolated area, contended for by the nobles of Ferrara, Lucca and Florence. Today it is a favorite among tourists, offering an atypical experience of Tuscany, with its oak and pine woods, chestnut groves, castles and fortress towns, watchtowers and crumbling churches. In addition to its lovely landscapes, Garfagnana is also esteemed for its authentic food and wine traditions, rich with local products that tell of a past marked by deprivation and inventiveness.

Garfagnana has strong ties with farro, arguably its most characteristic product. Though in the past considered a "poor" food, today farro is a prized export product throughout the world and had garnered much appreciation. Along with farro, chestnuts, the corn known as *formenton otto file* and other forest items like mushrooms and game have sustained this population for centuries.

Cured meats are part of the local cuisine as well, and a source of great pride among butchers. The blood sausage *biroldo*, now a Slow Food presidium, is perhaps the most emblematic of the tradition. Before letting the ingredients disturb you, try *biroldo* on a slice of grilled bread. Only afterwards ask how it's made.

The ingredients were explained to me at the Bellandi butchery shop, run by four generations of butchers and in business since just after World War II. They are located at the foot of the Apuane Alps in the Serchio Valley, where vast chestnut woods and stepped lands of cultivated farro bear witness to the ancient rural traditions of this area.

So, for the curious (and not squeamish), here are the ingredients: pig's head and cheek, offal and blood. The pork pieces are cooked for six hours, boned and seasoned, then added to the blood to be cooked another three hours in a pig's bladder. Before it would have been made at home, requiring a good deal of time of the household women who typically prepared it.

Another cured meat specialty here is the prosciutto called *bazzone*, also a Slow Food presidium, which is left to cure for as long as five years. *Manzo di pozza*, on the other hand, is marinated for 30 days with herbs, resulting in a cured meat similar to bresaola, while linchetto is sliced sirloin steak seasoned with dried porcini mushrooms.

Castelnuovo di Garfagnana

WHERE: The Piazza del Mercato and historic town center, Castelnuovo di Garfagnana.

WHEN: Thursday mornings.

NOT TO MISS: The traditional local cheeses from Contipelli and the Casciana apples.

WHERE TO HAVE BREAKFAST: At the Antica Pasticceria Fronte della Rocca, in business in Castelnuovo's Piazzetta Ariosto since 1885. Try one of their croissants made with organic heritage flours or taste some of their chocolate creations.

WHERE TO EAT: Try the fresh chestnut flour pasta with walnut sauce at Il Baretto, located at Via Farini 5. Or head to Osteria Il Vecchio Mulino to savor the authentic flavors of Garfagnana.

FOR GELATO: Stop by the gelateria Fuori dal Centro located on Via Olinto Dini, where the proprietors once served a gelato inspired by my recipe for Tuscan *cavallucci* cookies.

OUTSIDE THE MARKET: The Marovelli Formaggeria for local cheeses, chestnut and *formenton otto file* corn flours, and craft spelt and chestnut beers. You'll find even more area specialties at the old-fashioned shop L'Aia di Piero.

Castelnuovo is the regional capital of Garfagnana, and its most representative town. This is an area that has seen its fair share of history, from foreign rule and various battles to bandits, tradespeople and farmers, the noted short-term resident figure Ludovico Ariosto, and Pascoli and his family.

"Prepare yourself." This is what Annarita said to me when we made a plan to meet in Castelnuovo di Garfagnana, where a Thursday morning outdoor market has been running since 1430. Authentic, with ancient origins, this market seems straight out of the past, with scenes of elderly men sporting their hats and coats, and women who have spruced themselves up to browse the stands.

Like any classic Italian weekly market, there's a bit of everything here. Yet the most interesting feature is how the market is set up, winding through the narrow streets of town, up and down through its alleyways and small squares.

Among the various fruit and vegetable stands, you'll find the famous Casciana apples (when in season), a sour variety with very firm flesh that conserve well in winter. Locally grown potatoes and walnuts are also on offer, and of course there are the cheese stands, too. The cheeses from the Contipelli farm include top quality pecorino and a super fresh ricotta that can be enjoyed on its own or served with a dusting of sugar or salt. It's lovely as a filling in savory quiches or in the exquisite local specialty cake of Garfagnana.

Once you've seen the market, stop in at the Marovelli cheese shop to learn about one of Garfagnana's foremost products. In addition to pecorino cheese, Marovelli offers cow and goat milk cheese along with countless other specialty items.

FARINA DI
FARRO
FAGIOLI
CORONA
FAGIOLI NERI
~BLACK BEANS
€3,50/Kg.
ROSSONI
€4,50/Kg.

Barga

WHERE: Piazza Pascoli e Piazzale Matteotti, Barga.

WHEN: Saturday morning, from 8am to 1pm.

NOT TO MISS: The cheeses and cured meats at Casa del Formaggio.

WHERE TO HAVE BREAKFAST: The Fratelli Lucchesi pastry shop located in Piazzale Matteotti. They offer an incredible selection of croissants, tartlets and cookies, and in winter their panettone cakes and *befanini* cookies (frosted sugar cookies made for The Feast of the Epiphany, or *La Befana*).

WHERE TO EAT: At Trattoria l'Altana, located in the historic center of Barga, for great honest food.

Technically speaking, Barga is not part of Garfagnana but rather nearby in the Serchio Valley. Still, it's a perfect base for exploring this region, in any season. Barga has been granted recognition as one of the most beautiful villages in Italy. And rightly so. The best way to discover Barga is on foot, wandering through its narrow, hilly streets, passing the old town walls to take in lovely views, and climbing up to the cathedral that overlooks the entire town.

We visited Barga with Alessandro Manfredini, a Barga native who in addition to being a connoisseur of local cuisine is also a Tuscany-based Renaissance chef and cooking teacher. It was Alessandro who told us about the surprising link between Barga and Scotland.
In the post-war period, numerous inhabitants of Barga emigrated to Scotland to seek their fortunes.
Many of these opened fish and chip shops, and settled in that far away land.
Today almost everyone in Barga has a relative who lives in Scotland, relatives who return to Italy from time to time to visit family here. The family of the young Scottish singer Paolo Nutini has roots in Barga, which he visits every year for a few weeks in summer. There's even a Scottish phone booth in the middle of town, today a bookcrossing zone.

Before heading to the market, stop in at Caffè da Aristo in the upper part of old Barga. Opened in 1902, Aristo is a social hub where locals enjoy roasted chestnuts (when in season), live music and excellent craft beers. It's also great for a coffee, breakfast or a snack.

At the market you'll find not just fruit and vegetables but also a vast selection of local cheeses and cured meats, regional fresh pastas, dried mushrooms from the surrounding hillside, jams and marmalades, and of course potato bread.

PISTOIA, PRATO AND MONTECATINI

Until 1928, Pistoia was under the protective shadow of neighboring Florence. Today it is still influenced by the Tosco-Emiliano Apennine mountains, a poor area whose sustenance has long relied on chestnuts and polenta. Florence-dazzled tourists often overlook graceful, fascinating Pistoia, which, though quieter, boasts one of the loveliest market squares in all of Tuscany.

When the summer heat takes hold of the city, locals retreat to the forested slopes and chestnut groves of nearby Abetone Mountain. I first visited this popular winter holiday destination on a trip with my parents (I was too young to remember much of it, in truth, aside from seeing Santa Claus on skis). In summertime, berry bushes cover the slopes of Abetone, stretched out as far as the eye can see.

Not far from Pistoia in the middle of Valdinievole lies Montecatini, a thermal spa resort town that saw its golden age during the Belle Époque period. Famous throughout Europe and frequented by members of high society, Montecatini was beloved by illustrious figures and musicians, such as Verdi, Rossini, Leoncavallo, Puccini and Mascagni.

Today Montecatini feels almost like a seaside retreat, despite its only nearby water coming from the spas inside the various inns and small, luxury hotels along the peaceful, tree-lined boulevards. The spas continue to attract tourists interested in wellness holidays, yet Montecatini is also a perfect base for tourists wishing to explore this part of Tuscany, given its proximity to cities like Lucca, Pistoia and Florence.

Not far from here is the Italian capital of manufacturing and textiles, Prato, an ever-evolving industrial city that contributed significantly to the economic recovery of Italy in the post-war years. Located between Florence and Bologna, between the sea and the Apennine mountains, the Prato area is full of surprises. More than merely an industrial and urban center famous for its textiles, Prato also boasts museums, soft rolling hills covered in vineyards and olive groves, wine cellars and historic Medici villas. Starting with almond biscotti, Prato offers a rich array of traditional products and a strong local food culture.

Nearby Carmignano, for instance, produces quality wines using methods dating to the time of Cosimo III de' Medici. The thriving local pastry industry accounts for not only the well-known almond biscotti but also the almond cake *mantovana*, the Italian peach-shaped pastries called *le pesche*, anise-flavored cookies known as *zuccherini di Vernio*, Carmignano amaretto cookies and Calvana sassi cookies.

The markets here reflect this region's passion for quality, well-made food, the Saturday morning Terre di Prato market being a good example.

OROLOGI D'EPOCA
PANERAI

Pistoia, Piazza della Sala Market

WHERE: Piazza della Sala, Pistoia.

WHEN: Daily, with schedules varying with the seasons.

NOT TO MISS: The Banco del Gusto, da Montale and the shop run by Assunta.

WHERE TO EAT: In Piazza della Sala and along surrounding roads there's a remarkable selection to choose from. Try Trattoria Fiaschetteria La Pace.

WHERE TO STAY: Locanda San Marco, located at Via Porta S. Marco 26, is an elegant and welcoming inn located at the heart of the city, inside the late 17th-century Palazzo Caluri.

OUTSIDE THE MARKET: The Bruno Corsini *confetti* (almond candy) shop located at Piazza San Francesco 42. *Confetti* were a medieval specialty and past-time associated with festivity, much like the Santa Brigida cookies known as i *brigidini*.

Piazza della Sala has always been Pistoia's business and exchange center. It takes its name from the Sala, palace seat of the governing official during the Lombard era known as the gastald. Just next to Piazza del Duomo, the palace embodies a contrast between the commercial and secular aspects of local life and those religious in nature. The names of piazzas and alleyways that surround Piazza della Sala testify to a past marked by craft industries: Piazza dell'Ortaggio (garden square), Vicolo del Cacio (cheese alley), Via dei Fabbri (backsmiths' street), Via degli Orafi (goldsmiths' street), Sdrucciolo dei Cipollini (little onion alleyway), Via del Lastrone (stone slab street, from the large stones upon which fish vendors set up their wares) and Via di Stracceria (bric-a-brac street).
Today the fruit and vegetable stands occupy the center of the square, set up under large white tents that provide shelter from both the hot summer sun and winter storms.

At the edge of the piazza is the Banco del Gusto, in business since the 1980s, whose proud owners sell particularly tender home-grown zucchini (seeded annually for generations).
Some years back there was an elderly woman here whom I never had the chance to meet. Still remembered by those who frequent the market, Primetta sold eggs and the wild herbs she foraged, including the mysterious plant known as *erba della paura*, or "fear's herb" (*Stachys recta*; commonly called hedge-nettle). Every herb had a function, whether culinary or magical. Numerous crafts and food shops line the piazza and surrounding roads: bakeries, butcher and deli shops, and a hardware store carrying a vast range of merchandise.
In the middle of all this stands Sauro Signori's fruit and vegetable shop. Here you can find excellent local produce, from the meraviglia green beans to asparagus from the Albinatico area. Their unusually labelled products include zucchini "picked early this morning by Mario" and Capezzano beans "creamy as silk." They also offer a selection of Italian legumes and flours, in particular flours used for polenta.
On winter evenings this market stays open later, with stands starting to close down a little after 7pm. Wandering around a market in the dark is quite an unusual experience: the piazza seems to envelop you in its warmth, fostering an even more intimate connection with the vendors behind their stands.
As soon as the market shuts down, Piazza della Sala's many bars, osterias and restaurants begin to fill up, transforming the square into the center of Pistoia's nightlife.

FRAGOLE
SICILIA
MELOGRANE
PIRACCINI

CIALDE

Montecatini Earth Market

WHERE: Via Mazzini, Montecatini.

WHEN: Saturday morning, from 8am to 1pm.

NOT TO MISS: The *cinta senese* cured pork products and the pecorino cheese from Lenzini farm.

WHERE TO HAVE A DRINK: At Caffè Giusti in Piazza Giusti 25 in Montecatini Alta (upper Montecatini).

WHERE TO EAT: At La Pecora Nera at Via S. Martino 18. La Pecora Nera is an elegant yet informal place with a homey feel, suited to everyone. The atmosphere is bright and cozy, and in summer you can eat outside on the terrace under the shade of climbing plants. The fish dishes here are renowned.

WHERE TO STAY: At Hotel Natucci at Via Felice Cavallotti 102 for a warm and simple, authentic dinner.

OUTSIDE THE MARKET: Try the wafer cookies at Montecatini del Bargilli on Viale Pietro Grocco. And be sure to make time for a few hours at one of the spas, an experience even more worthwhile given the splendid Belle Époque setting.

Montecatini's golden age was at the start of the 20th century, and today it still retains an air of elegance thanks to its various spa resorts and luxury hotels in Belle Époque style. Slow Food's Mercato della Terra, or Earth Market, is housed in a fascinating semi-enclosed structure from this period, the seat of the city's historic farmers market.

Here you will find fruit, vegetables, honeys, cheeses, breads and organic flours, legumes, oil, craft beers and local wines, fresh pasta, jams and artisanal cookies. The meat selection is rather vast for a farmers market, which tends to focus more on fruit and vegetables. There are *cinta senese* pork products, including *scamerita* (capocollo), *rigatino* (similar to pancetta), *coppa* (a raw salami made from pig neck and shoulder) as well as sausages, broth bones, prosciutto, salami, rolled pancetta, and chickens and rabbits from Corazzano San Miniato. A kind woman named Franca brings sauces to the market from the Nonna Olga Farm in Monsummano Terme, including jams, fruit and vegetable sauces, canned fruit and vegetables—all made with her homegrown items from the veggie patch and fruit orchards.

The Lenzini Farm of Borgo a Buggiano, on the other hand, offers a variety of fresh milk products delivered from the Pistoia Mountains: raw milk pecorino (a Slow Food Presidium), soft and aged sheep and cow milk cheeses, milk, ricotta, yogurt, and panna cotta for those with a sweet tooth. In compliance with Slow Food statutes, everything here is seasonal and traceable. Producers are local, coming from the Valdinievole and surrounding areas, and always eager to chat with customers and share interesting tidbits of information. These are relationships that go well beyond mere commercial exchange.

The Earth Market is a multi-functional event, a place to do the shopping, to meet up with others, and to discover various local products, some nearly forgotten. Here you can mark the changing of the seasons based on the rotation of products available. From time to time, producers will also organize tastings and workshops for children and adults, much in the spirit of a market dedicated to highlighting the important role of local producers.

Prato

WHERE: Piazza del Mercato Nuovo, Prato.

WHEN: Saturday morning, from 8am to 1pm.

NOT TO MISS: The Prato mortadella and wurstel (Vienna sausages) at Salumeria Mannori, the GranPrato flour, and the bread and schiacciata from Panificio Cocciardi.

WHERE TO EAT: At Il Dek Italian Bistrot, located at Piazza delle Carceri 1/2, for pizza, sandwiches and traditional and modern dishes.

WHERE TO STOP FOR A SWEET SNACK: Pasticceria Fiaschi in Piazza Mercatale for their freshly made *bomboloni*, fried donuts filled with cream, chocolate, or jam (available until evening). Paolo Sacchetti's café and pastry shop Nuovo Mondo, located at Via Garibaldi 23, for their famous Prato *pesche* (peach-shaped pastries filled with cream and infused with liqueurs).

OUTSIDE THE MARKET: Head to Biscottificio Mattei on Via Ricasoli for their now-classic Prato almond biscotti.

This market, one of Tuscany's finest, is held in a parking lot a little outside the town center, surrounded by tall trees, warehouses and other industrial buildings. The setting is one of lively, modern contrasts. As you make your way towards the Terra di Prato's market stands, you start to sense the buzz of activity—the comings and goings of shoppers, the variety of products on offer, the gratifying smells in the air that lure you onwards.

Every now and then, a market offering excellent bread comes along, as well as a chance to pick up wonderful breads baked in wood-fired ovens and stone-ground flours made from local heritage grains. These markets fill me with hope for a better future, one in which flours are less refined, and the breads made from them emit the genuine fragrance of wheat and taste as they truly should.

Since 2011, the GranPrato flour-making initiative has been promoting Prato's supply chain of local grains, with the goal of sustaining area agriculture and fostering appreciation of one of the pillars of Prato food production, breads and baked goods, including *la bozza pratese* (a rectangular, peasant style bread), *biscotti*, and the *mantovana* cake from Mattei bakery (a simple cake noted by Pellegrino Artusi).

Also well represented at this market are seasonal fruit and vegetables, whose vendors have no need to holler at passersby: their products speak for themselves, from vibrant pumpkins in winter to fresh, aromatic strawberries in summer.

Next are the soft and aged pecorino cheeses, fresh pasta, cured meats, the local variety of Prato mortadella made by Mannori, and the Calvana breed beef—a native Tuscan breed of cattle related to Chianina, once widespread throughout the Tuscan Apennine mountains and today limited to a few areas between the Calvana mountains and the Mugello, east of Prato.

MUGELLO
The Garden of Florence

Until a few years ago, I thought of the Mugello region as simply the place that produced the good milk I was raised on. Then I met Tommaso, who over the course of a year became first one of my best friends and then my life partner. His family is from Mugello, and he grew up there until the age of 12 when the family moved to Florence.

Our first countryside outings together were here. We went to the town of Scarperia for the sagra dei tortelli, a food festival dedicated to a type of potato-filled pasta similar to ravioli. We also visited the Monte Senario Sanctuary near Bivigliano, and headed up to the Futa Pass in early spring to enjoy the season's last snow.

As we toured the area, he showed me the fields, valleys, pine woods and chestnut groves with pride, along with the Medici villas and small hamlets that seemed like snapshots frozen in time.
This is one of the least known parts of Tuscany, yet Florentines have long prized it as the perfect escape from their city's unbearable summer humidity. They come for the clean air, country walks and authentic food found throughout these hills, valleys and mountains.
Vasari called this area "the garden of Florence."

The Medici family originated here in the town of Cafaggiolo and maintained strong ties with this part of Tuscany, even more so than with Chianti. They built hunting lodges, villas and fortresses across the region, including their first hunting reserve in Pratolino. The Medici also managed experimental farms, importing Alpine cattle breeds from Switzerland and setting up a dairy farm they called Panna.

Bordering Emilia-Romagna and Florence, Mugello bears the influences of both its neighbors in its cuisine, reinterpreting them with the help of local products like potatoes, chestnuts, mushrooms and other forest products, meat and game, milk and cheeses.

The Mugello area is easily reachable from Florence by quick and direct routes, or, if you're up for a fun ride, via the windy county roads so beloved by motorcyclists for the lovely valleys and forested landscapes. Otherwise you can get there by train, along the old rail line that connects Florence to Faenza and passes through several Mugello towns and villages: Vaglia, San Piero a Sieve, Borgo San Lorenzo, Ronta, Marradi, and Palazzuolo sul Senio (from where you can enter the Emilia-Romagna region and visit San Cassiano and Brisighella as well). It's a relaxing, old-fashioned way of travelling, marked by the changing landscapes seen through the train car windows as you leave the city behind and head into the woods.

An alternative way to explore Mugello is to follow its "Via del Latte" or "Milk Road," an initiative of the Mukki dairy company. This touristic itinerary connects the region's 29 dairy and cattle farms that today produce Mukki's two local milks, Selezione Mugello and Podere Centrale.

Borgo San Lorenzo

WHERE: Borgo San Lorenzo center.

WHEN: Tuesday mornings, from 8am to 1pm.

NOT TO MISS: The meats at the CAF Cooperativa Agricola Firenzuola.

WHERE TO EAT: Stop by Passaguai located at Piazza Garibaldi 2, a restaurant, enoteca, cocktail bar and deli.

WHERE TO STOP FOR A SWEET SNACK: Pasticceria Aurelio at Via D. Partigiana Garibaldi 5, to try the *panmarrone del Mugello* (similar to panettone, made with chestnut flour and marrons glacés), the *zuccotto* and the *torta in balconata*, a tiered cake made according to a 15th-century Medici court recipe.

OUTSIDE THE MARKET: Try the tortelli at Pastificio San Lorenzo located at Via dell'Artigianato 6/8 Loc. Rabatta.

Borgo San Lorenzo's weekly market coincides with the Mugello farmers market. Here you'll find a selection of local seasonal fruit and vegetables, everything from potatoes for *tortelli* to mushrooms and chestnuts. A range of local sheep and cow milk cheeses is also on offer. Yet the absolute must-see is the tripe vendor from Florence with its aromas of *lampredotto*, tripe, *nervetti* (tendons), *musetto* (sausage made from various pig's head pieces), *matrice* (boiled cow uterus) and *poppa* (cured cow udder).

The liveliest stand is CAF, the Cooperativa Agricola Firenzuola, and not only on account of the entertaining and jovial butcher. All the meats sold here come from cows, sheep and pigs raised by the members of the Cooperative who guarantee the highest quality of all their cuts. Naturally, you will find classic cuts like Florentine t-bone steak and fillets, along with *musetto* sausage and *guancia* (cheek) for traditional slow-cooked dishes. CAF also sells honeys, grains, legumes, fresh pasta and cured meats.
Browsing the homeware stands you'll find pasta cutters for making *tortelli*, stuffed pasta similar to ravioli. Ask around for the best place to eat Mugello *tortelli*. The list of options will be long, yet the names that come up most frequently are da Giorgione in Sagginale, the Casa del Prosciutto in Ponte a Vicchio, and the bar and pizzeria Valeri in Luco di Mugello. Otherwise, another option is to head to one of the local *sagre* (food fairs) held in small towns throughout the area. The *sagra* custom sees local women coming together to work, forming an assembly line to produce shocking amounts of tortelli that are then readily (and quickly) consumed by local residents, tourists and Florentines fleeing the city heat.

In Borgo San Lorenzo you can also purchase pre-made *tortelli* at Pastificio San Lorenzo.
Note that asking a Mugello local how to make tortelli is akin to asking her to reveal the secrets of the Holy Grail. The base ingredient is always potato, yet the rest varies, from those who add garlic or parsley to those who swear that a hint of tomato paste or spoonful of meat sauce is needed for the filling. In Palazzuolo sul Senio the custom is to add a bit of ricotta, a bold touch that reflects the influence of neighboring Romagna. The most memorable I've tried were filled with potato, leek, garlic and cheese.
Tortelli are typically served with a hearty meat ragù, wild boar sauce or duck meat sauce. But at a *sagra* you will also see them served with butter and sage, pesto or tomato sauce.

MARRONI
DI
MARRADI
TRATTATI
€6.00
K

Marradi

WHERE: Marradi town center.

WHEN: Usually every Sunday in October.

NOT TO MISS: Be sure to stock up on the fresh, lovely chestnuts available here.

WHERE TO HAVE LUNCH: Have a sandwich made with local cured meats or polenta with meat sauce, and of course some pastries to follow—all available at the market stands. No one comes away from this market hungry.

WHERE TO STOP FOR A SWEET SNACK: Chestnut products abound here. Stop by Forno Sartoni located at Via Fabbrini 22 for their *castagnaccio*, chestnut cakes, cookies and other tarts; or at the Forno Bellini and pastry shop for the fried tortellini, the chestnut Swiss rolls and puddings.

OUTSIDE THE MARKET: From Marradi you can head to Palazzuolo sul Senio, which holds a similar market on the same days.

Strictly speaking, this is not a farmers market, but rather a festival dedicated to Marradi's renowned chestnuts. Running for some 50 years now, this event attracts folks from all over Tuscany and Emilia-Romagna on Sundays in October.
Visitors arrive in hoards and the town center fills up with stands and counters where you will find not only chestnuts—arranged in every possible manner—but also crates of apples, Volpina pears and other forgotten fruits, towers of local cheeses like pecorino aged in chestnut or walnut leaves, truffles and local mushrooms, from fragrant porcini to the precious ovoli variety (*Amanita caesarea*), porchetta, tripe, *lampredotto* or cured meat sandwiches, and plenty of other traditional dishes.

Chestnuts are the unrivaled king of this scene. Gathered in enormous containers along the town's small streets and alleyways, these shiny round nuts are the truest symbol of fall in the Mugello woods. Choose between *castagne*, or regular chestnuts, and *marroni*, a sweet and delicate local variety. The choice should be based on how you intend to use them—Roasted? Or in recipes? And of course you can always pick up dried and other processed chestnuts, too. For instance, *marroni* chestnuts can be covered in water, usually in huge wooden or plastic containers, to soak for several days and then dry out again. This method removes all the aerobic bacteria and mold agents, guaranteeing a longer shelf-life.
The range of chestnut products is astounding, from flours and creams and the floury and very sweet roasted chestnuts with their burnt bits here and there to chestnut brittle, marrons glacés, and caramel-covered chestnuts on skewers. All of these alongside the traditional *castagnaccio* and other cakes typical of Marradi, Swiss rolls made with sponge cake, Alchermes and chestnut cream, chestnut flour crêpes and *tortelli* pasta. Every kind of sweet or salty chestnut delicacy imaginable is on show here, all made according to recipes that live on in local memory.
There are plenty of chances to drink well at this festival, too. Alongside chestnut beers are the local wines Ciliegiolo and Cagnina, a sweet "young" wine drunk during festive periods in the Romagna area that goes very well with roasted chestnuts. In October, those heading to Marradi's chestnut festival can take a special vintage train service to get them in the appropriate "retro" mood.

LUCCA AND VERSILIA

I discovered Lucca and Versilia as an adult. The first time I saw Lucca it was a Saturday afternoon, a little before Christmas. I had no idea what Lucca's historical city center was like, and I had not imagined it would have the classic narrow streets typical of medieval towns. I was meant to be there by 6pm for a work meeting at a hotel. The hotel had said I could leave my car in their garage, so without a second thought I drove into the town's center.

I soon found myself surrounded by folks taking their evening stroll, well-dressed families finishing their Christmas shopping in the crowded shops... soon the colors, lights and decorations began to muddle my vision.

Defeated, I exited the city center as soon as I could and left my car in a parking lot outside the town's walls. I still recall the atmosphere that Saturday afternoon, with the city dressed in its festive best, the brilliant shops and gorgeous window fronts. Every time I go back to Lucca that festive feeling is with me, even if we're there in the middle of summer, perhaps because of its lively and orderly streets, the restaurants lining them or tucked away in shady gardens. What really made me fall in love with Lucca, though, was the four-kilometer walk along the city walls that encircle the town. The views from atop this tree-lined walled circle, the second largest of its kind in Europe, offer a peek into the town's tiny alleyways, shady piazzas and internal courtyards.

Versilia, on the other hand, famous for its association with Viareggio's Carnival, was unknown to me for many years. I always thought of that festivity as the final obstacle between me and the arrival of spring. Carnival, with its colorful confetti, streamers and amazing costumes, meant enduring the last dull days before the rebirth of the new season. As a food lover, I admit I was taken in by the sweets associated with this festival, to me the only positive thing about this particular moment in the year: *frittelle* (sweet fritters), *cenci* (fried and sugared dough strips) and *schiacciata fiorentina* (a sponge cake topped with powdered sugar).

But then came a chance to experience a Carnival weekend in Viareggio and discover some of the amazing elements of this tradition: the impressive engineering behind the large floats, for example, along with the risottos and fried foods at the Carnevaldarsena festival, the wholesome fun of the parades and various districts, the true and genuine passion of those who observe Carnival as one of the most important moments of the year. And I changed my mind.

For the people of Viareggio, Carnival is not at all an obstacle but rather a passageway to the season of spring. After a winter of harsh weather and little activity, Carnival is the beginning of a seasonal rebirth that will take us into summer, when sun and sea, work and tourism reign. It took this subtle change in perspective to shake up my notion of Carnival and to broaden my appreciation of Versilia.

JOTUN
VGMARIA
3548

Illuminati frutta
POMODORO
CANESTRINO
2,50€/Kg

Lucca, the Farmers Market at the Ancient Forum Boarium

WHERE: The Foro Boario structure in Lucca.

WHEN: Saturday morning, from 8am to 1pm.

NOT TO MISS: The fresh milk vending machine, the local beach honey and the fresh vegetables from the Calafata farm.

WHERE TO EAT: At Trattoria Canuleia located at Via Canuleia 14, with its lovely internal garden, perfect for summer nights. Or at Gli Orti di Via Elisa Restaurant at Via Elisa 17, where you'll find traditional Lucca dishes and local products.

OUTSIDE THE MARKET: Try the *buccellato*, the local bread-like round cake studded with raisins at Taddeucci pastry shop, an elegant bakery in business since 1881. Looking a bit like an old-fashioned general store, with huge window fronts full of sweets and cakes, Taddeucci is located right in Lucca's city center in Piazza San Michele, next to the church of the same name.

Lucca's farmers market takes place just outside the historic town center at the structure called Foro Boario, not far from the Serchio river. Under its shady awnings that protect against summer's infernal heat, Lucca's short supply chain farmers bring the best the season has to offer to the market.

While travelling around Tuscany (and beyond), I have visited numerous farmers markets, but this one truly won me over with its impressive variety of garden fruits and vegetables. Take eggplant, for instance. Here you'll find oblong, white, purple and striped varieties. This market offers chard with colorful stalks, carrots with their greens still attached, kale in splendid shades of blue and tomatoes still warm from the sun.

Red and yellow new potatoes still smudged with the dirt from which they came—is there a better sign of harvest quality?—are arranged in paper sacks with rosemary, ready for Sunday's roast.
All of this reflects the dedicated passion with which these farmers protect ancient varieties, to bring to their market stands not just flavor, but flavors recovered from the past.

Alongside the plentiful and colorful fruits and vegetables are stands offering fish from the nearby coasts, meats, local cheeses, extra virgin olive oil, wine and honey.
One of the characteristic products of Tuscany's farmers markets is honey, available here in several varieties, including a locally made beach honey.
This is a small-production, organic honey that stays liquid through the end of summer before naturally crystallizing in the fall. Its aroma recalls warm, sea-salty winds, which makes it perfect for spreading on bread with butter. Pair it with aged cheeses or use it to dress certain types of salads.

Before leaving the market, stop at the entrance to buy fresh, unpasteurized milk from the automatic vending machine, produced by the Lammari farm.

Camaiore

WHERE: Via Oberdan, Camaiore.

WHEN: Friday morning.

NOT TO MISS: The pink lardo and other products at the Gombitelli deli shop.

WHERE TO HAVE BREAKFAST: Stop at the Pasticceria Rossano at Via Stadio 39 for a cappuccino or coffee with a croissant that's as tasty as it is huge!

WHERE TO EAT: At Locanda Le Monache restaurant, a rustic locale in business since 1923, where you can taste some of the best Camaiore *tordelli*. Located at Piazza XXIX Maggio 36.

OUTSIDE THE MARKET: Head to Osteria Candalla, located a little outside the Camaiore town center at Via di Candalla 246, in Lobrici. Here you will find the best *tordelli* around, a traditional homemade Tuscan pasta, while inside a former water mill situated on a small creek.

Camaiore lies between the sea and the mountains, between the Lido beaches beloved by Gabriele D'Annunzio and Eleonora Duse and the Apuan Alps with their enchanting, gradual descent from the Mediterranean maquis to Alpine pastures.

The first documentation of a market fair in Camaiore dates to All Saints' Day, 1437. In the 15th century, celebrations of this day lasted from the end of October to the start of November, whereas today the observance is limited to the first and second day of November. On this occasion, the town's streets and piazzas fill up with food and clothing stands, much like our classic Italian markets.

The weekly market, on the other hand, is set up along the streets of Camaiore every Friday morning.

After passing the clothing stands, then next thing you'll notice is the aroma of Cinta prosciutto, cheese and porchetta. A few vegetable stands later and you'll arrive at Gombitelli, representatives of the ancient *norcineria* tradition—pork butchery and cured pork meats—who lure market-goers with their lovely local salamis and cured meats. Here you will also find excellent, naturally leavened Tuscan bread, creamed lardo spread with spices, cured meats such as aged *arista* (pork loin), rolled lardo and cheeses, in particular pecorino cheeses. But the star of the Gombitelli stand is undoubtedly their pink lardo.

PRESCIUTTO
di CINTA
€70,00
ARROSTO
di GRANO
COTTO
della ZIA

Viareggio, the Fish Market on the Pier

WHERE: On the Viareggio pier.

WHEN: Every morning.

NOT TO MISS: The freshly caught fish, naturally. Get there early to find the best selection..

WHERE TO EAT: At Tito del Molo on Viale Regina Margherita, famous for its grilled and fried fish dishes.

OUTSIDE THE MARKET: Get out and enjoy the sea while catching super fresh fish with Moreno and Enrico of Mas 500, located along the Darsena Toscana in Piazzale Don Sirio Politi.

The fishing vessels dock around 10am in Viareggio, delivering the previous night's catch of fresh fish to the stands along the pier.

You can easily recognize which of these colorful, chatty and able merchants are the fishermen as they hang around behind each stand. Dealings with fishermen here are straightforward. While some might offer market prices considerably lower than those of a regular fish shop, the negotiating calls for skill and experience as well as the ability to distinguish the quality of the fish.

The selection is limited compared to what you would find at a fish shop, owing to the fact that everything sold along the pier is fished just hours before. Nothing could be more local, seasonal and sustainable.

Further on are the stalls run by the Mare Nostrum cooperative, another recommended place for buying excellent fresh fish and a good choice for non-experts like myself. This is where I ran into Moreno Pellegrini.

Moreno is not just a fisherman. He also organizes fishing trips for tourists, taking sea- and fish-lovers on a unique experience on his boat. The day's catch becomes the meal, prepared in Moreno's very small yet nicely equipped kitchen (it made me rethink my views on small spaces, actually).

My experience in Viareggio turned out to be one of the most meaningful of my journey through Tuscany's markets. Moreno added some chairs to the table on his boat, then squeezed into this tiny kitchen and invited us to lunch. Between the hypnotic rolling of the sea and aroma of garlic and oil filling the air, I spent a few hours watching the secrets of seafood cooking unveil before my eyes: the highest quality fresh fish, quick cooking times and, per Moreno, a grating of lemon zest to lend that extra special touch to every dish.

V.G. 3407
MP.ANTONINA
VG 3407

DYNAMIC
23
Dark age of fantasy

Viareggio's Indoor Market

WHERE: Piazza Cavour, Viareggio.

WHEN: Daily.

NOT TO MISS: L'Acciuga fish shop for a quick lunch from the day's catch.

WHERE TO STOP FOR A SWEET SNACK: At the Pasticceria Patalani at Via Giuseppe Zanardelli 183, where the tradition and craft of pastry making reign. Be sure to try the soft and fluffy mini *bomboloni* made with sourdough starter.

OUTSIDE THE MARKET: The Viareggio Carnival is something that everyone, young or old, should experience. Join in the Carnevaldarsena, get lost in the celebratory crowds and enjoy dinner in this town quarter.

I wandered these streets for years, unaware that behind the bric-a-brac, games, and wicker objects stands hid Viareggio's indoor market.

When I first started teaching cooking classes, back before I opened my home to tourists from around the world, I used to come to Viareggio once a month, to a marvelous homeware shop to give cooking demonstrations. I was like a child in a toy shop. Gradually this became a regular appointment, one I grew rather fond of. A group of customers loyal to the shop would return every time, either to make Christmas cookies or fresh pasta, or to venture with me into my world of international recipes. Firstly, these people trusted me. They believed in me and in my passion, showing me with their encouraging smiles and full mouths that cooking was truly my path in life. With them I learned how to check my anxiety and shaking voice when speaking: at first before ten people, then twenty, then thirty. There I learned the importance of being organized and not panicking when something goes wrong. There I exchanged so many recipes with women who came those Saturdays, from *befanini* cookies to the sweet zucchini tart known as *la scarpaccia*.

But let's get back to the indoor market in the heart of Viareggio. Here there is much more than fish, although do have a quick lunch at Pescheria l'Acciuga, something from the day's catch, if you can. Take a look at the meats from Michelangelo Masoni, a butcher famous for his scrupulous dedication when it comes to choosing his products. Born into a family of butchers in the business since 1920, he inherited his passion and precision from his father, who for years scoured the Tuscan countryside in search of the best meats. Today Michelangelo deals mostly in meats from the Piedmontese cattle breed.

At the Polleria del Popolo dei Fratelli Pertici poultry shop you can stock up on chicken, rabbit and game. Lastly, visit the Triglia salumeria for stocks of Gombitelli cured meats, the famous pink lardo, prosciutto, rolled pancetta, salami, sausages, cheeses, jams, sauces and other traditional local products.

PISA, SAN MINIATO AND VOLTERRA

Pisa is often the first Tuscan city tourists see, on account of its large international airport. For many of these visitors, Pisa means the space limited to Piazza dei Miracoli, a UNESCO World Heritage site since 1987 and home to the cathedral, baptistry, monumental cemetery and the Leaning Tower. And yet there is so much more to Pisa.

It's the only city I've lived in outside my home in the countryside. About ten years ago, I stayed in Pisa for five weeks to work as a class tutor. I discovered so many things during that time, including *cecina*, which I later came across again in Livorno, only under a different name.

In Pisa, I also discovered the freedom of doing my own shopping, of cooking dinner on my own with the help of just a microwave. That's right. In the rush and excitement of making that move, I ended up taking a small house near the school where the lessons were held—only to realize after moving in that it did not have a proper kitchen! Yet somehow those steamed vegetables and reheated dinners tasted of independence and adulthood.

Walking the streets of Pisa, you can't help but feel the excitement in the air, a buzz that only a university town can generate with its bars, stores, countless bookshops, and markets, too.

Pisa is not very far from my home, actually. I live in a corner of the Siena province that is very close to both the provinces of Florence (near Val d'Elsa) and Pisa. Heading towards the sea from my place, after about a half hour of windy roads and wild hills, you come to the *Volterrano*, the area around Volterra. With its independent, anarchic character, its traditional cuisine and more, the Volterrano emits an aura of mystery inherited from its first inhabitants, the Etruscans.

Having turned its isolated location into a strength, Volterra continues to attract tourists from around the world as a livable, friendly city. Here, local residents frequent the artisan shops in the town center, where every Sunday morning they stop to pick up lightly sugared, cream-filled pastries to take home for lunch with the family. Here, bars and Arci *circoli* (a *circolo* is a cultural and recreational center, similar to a social club) are still popular meeting places for young and old alike.

Volterra has been known for ages for its alabaster carving craft tradition, still evident today in the fine white powder seen dusting its cobblestone streets, the same powder that transforms local artisan work spaces into surreally lunar scenes.

Kg
italiana macchi
ITALIANA
MACCHI

Pisa, the Farmers Market in Piazza Santa Caterina

WHERE: Piazza Santa Caterina, Pisa.

WHEN: Every second and fourth Saturday of the month, excluding July and August.

NOT TO MISS: The various types of fresh pasta, flours and lardo sausage from the Biorialto farm.

WHERE TO STOP FOR A SNACK: At Il Montino pizzeria at Via Monte 1, a little-known spot where, in my opinion, they make the best *cecina* in Pisa, served with grilled eggplant.

WHERE TO HAVE GELATO: At Gelateria Naturale Artigianale De' Coltelli for some of the most delicious gelato I have ever tried, made with the highest quality fresh, seasonal, organic fruit, and no synthetic aromas, colors or preservatives of any kind. Definitely try their whipped cream!

On each trip to Pisa, I have often found myself passing by the market in Piazza delle Vettovaglie, a piazza whose name conveys its primary function (*vettovaglie* means "provisions"). The piazza is host every morning to the farmers market, where locals pick up fruit, vegetables and other food products, while the lively spaces under the surrounding porticoes are teeming with restaurants, enotecas, butcher shops, fish counters, bakeries and grocers. Today, though, there is one more farmers' market, which fills Piazza Santa Caterina with all kinds of activity, music, and some exuberant shouting.

Two Saturdays a month, producers from around the Pisan and greater Tuscan countryside come to market. These are small, family-run farms that have been practicing sustainable, organic farming, strictly pesticide-free, for years. Enjoy the selection of breads, flours, extra virgin olive oil, wine, local cheeses, honeys and jams, organic fruit, vegetables and legumes. Among the many stands, you are sure to notice the most vibrant of them all: the one capturing the attention of market-goers with its varied selection of pasta shapes and colors, made with different types of flour and colorings derived from spices and other natural ingredients.
Plenty of cured meats are on offer here, too, all made according to traditional Tuscan methods and following established curing periods. From the Biorialto farm, products from semi-free-range Cinta Senese pigs raised in the Quercianella hillside are sold at this market, from various fresh sausages (including lardo sausage) to *porchetta*, *sbriciolona*, prosciutto, coppa and salami.
Other products on hand at this market are artisan-produced essential oils, ecological soaps and fabrics. Each day has a theme, according to which market organizers host workshops for children and adults, such as natural fabric dying. Music is one of the more distinguishing aspects of this market: popular songs are accompanied by protest lyrics, fairy tales, peasants songs and workers' chants.
When the market closes down, large tables are set up in the middle of the piazza, where farmers and visitors are welcome to join in and share lunch. Bring something from home or, better still, purchase something from one of the producers to share.
After leaving the market, head to the historic pastry shop Salza, located at Borgo Stretto 46, where I usually have a coffee along with a *meringhetta alla panna* (small meringues with fresh cream). This is my Pisa ritual, along with a slice of *cecina* at Montino.

La Patata
Toscana

BOBO tipical
by Tuscany
TARTUFI E PRODOTTI AL TARTUFO
GRAPPE PARTICOLARI E SOUVENIR
DEGUSTAZIONE VINI LOCALI
www.bobotipical.com

San Miniato, the White Truffle Market Fair

WHERE: San Miniato's historic town center.

WHEN: Usually weekends in November.

NOT TO MISS: The white truffles of San Miniato, of course, but also the pork cheek pâté and truffle sausages from the Macelleria Sergio Falaschi, located at Via Augusto Conti 16. At Falaschi you can also have lunch or dinner.

WHERE TO EAT: Try the homemade pasta and white truffle recipes at Pepenero at Via 4 Novembre 13, a chic locale with a terrace with a view; or at the Prosciutteria at Via Ser Ridolfo 8 for the cheese and cold cuts platters, *lampredotto* and great sandwiches. The truffle mortadella sandwich is legendary.

WHERE TO STOP FOR A SWEET SNACK: Head to Il Cantuccio di Federigo at Via Paolo Maioli 67 for their fragrant *cantucci* cookies, filled with lightly toasted almonds and raisins.

San Miniato held its first Sagra del Tartufo, or Truffle Fair, in 1969 in its Piazza del Duomo. After a two-year hiatus, the fair started up again and has been ongoing ever since, and the growth and expansion of this popular fall event has brought international fame to the town.

While white truffles remain the stars of the show, over the years other local products have joined in, products that speak to the bonds between San Miniato and its surrounding territory. Wine, cheese, chestnuts and cured meats are all represented during these three November weekends, forming part of the truffle-themed backdrop: white and black truffles, truffle creams, and truffle oils and sauces.

Every year the fair awards prizes for the largest truffle and the oldest truffle hunter. The entire town gets involved, with roads and piazzas coming to life with food-themed events, workshops and presentations. Merchants display their products and restaurants plan truffle-based menus, while local associations set up refreshment stands for wayfarers, offering traditional dishes, nourishing and plentiful.

The beating heart of the fair is the Officina del Tartufo, the organizational space that hosts the onslaught of events and guests. During these weekends, waves of gourmets, foodies and tourists make their way to Piazza del Duomo, where stands displaying San Miniato white truffles, local wines and Italian specialties are set up. Stands highlighting the region's excellent agricultural food products are found in Piazza del Seminario and Piazza del Popolo.

Wandering around San Miniato for the truffle fair, be sure to stop at the Falaschi butchery shop, a meat-lover's temple producing cured meats according to traditional methods. Once inside, if you can resist the lure of the meats, pass through the shop until you reach the terrace with its stunning view of Tuscan vineyards, olive trees and rolling hills.

Volterra

WHERE: Piazza dei Priori in winter and Vallebuona (in front of the Roman theater) in summer.

WHEN: Every Saturday morning.

NOT TO MISS: The *mallegato* at Macelleria Franco & Luciana.

WHERE TO EAT: At La Carabaccia in Piazza XX Settembre for traditional Volterra dishes, from tagliatelle with pigeon to the migliacci crêpes cooked with pork broth.

WHERE TO STOP FOR A SNACK: For pizzas, focaccia and chickpea flatbread stop by the pizzeria Da Nanni at Via delle Prigioni 40.

OUTSIDE THE MARKET: Just before Volterra you'll find the Fattoria Lischeto, which started out as an agropastoral farm and is now an organic agritourism structure that makes cheeses, pasta and highest quality olive oil. Unlike the rural silence of the average agritourism structure, here you'll find contemporary art installations accompanied by the interesting surprises one expects whenever food and art are united.

Make your way to Volterra on a Saturday morning in winter. Go inside the Palazzo dei Priori, the oldest town hall in Tuscany. Climb the tower to peek out of the small windows. Likely you will glimpse Volterra enveloped in a dense, mysterious fog—one of its most fascinating traits—as you peer out onto the expanse of brick red and the colors of the lively market below. In wintertime, this market is held within the city's walls. Starting at Piazza dei Priori, the market weaves through streets and piazzas, taking up as much space from the civic Piazza dei Priori as it does from the religious sites in Piazza San Giovanni, the Duomo and Baptistery.

In spring and summer, on the other hand, the Volterra market takes place in Vallebuona, next to the historic marketplace. Here you will find seasonal fruit and vegetables, cheeses and salamis, a rotisserie stand, fish counters and a fry shop. Yet one of Volterra's most traditional products is not to be found at the market, but rather hidden along its stone streets and alleyways. You'll have to search out a local butcher to find the unique blood sausage called *mallegato*, beloved by Tuscans, who are known for their almost cult-like devotion to dishes made with stale bread. In its most classic form, San Miniato *mallegato* is made by encasing raw blood together with pieces of fat, salt, nutmeg, cinnamon, pine nuts and raisins. The casings are left a bit loose to prevent explosions during cooking, a technique from which *mallegato* takes its name, meaning something like "badly tied." The version made in Volterra is different, calling for the addition of stale bread that's been soaked in water, crumbled and reduced to a pulp. In the 18th century, *mallegato* was the typical breakfast of alabaster workers, men who needed a hearty yet economic breakfast.

Forgotten for a long while, *mallegato* has made a comeback and is today promoted as a traditional local product in spite of its somewhat unappealing appearance. Almost black in color, *mallegato* has a sweet and spicy aromatic flavor. *Mallegato* is sliced thickly, then breaded and fried, served perhaps alongside some bitter radicchio to contrast with its sweetness, or cooked with eggs just like *buristo*, another Tuscan cured meat similar to *mallegato*.

PROSCIUTTO CRUDO
NOSTRALE

Mai
2005
1
8
15
22
7
14
21

LEONARDO

IL MACCHIATINO

Volterra's Favorite Drink

This is the traditional beverage favored by Volterra's alabaster workers come the close of the work day. It's called *il macchiatino*. Forget afternoon tea or hot espresso. Nothing could be farther from the classic coffee break than this custom.

The ingredients here are of an entirely different kind, and what's more are alcoholic, calling for 4 parts white wine and 2 parts bitter Campari. Locals drink this specialty in a wine glass, known in Volterra as riparella. As the pre-meal aperitif of alabaster workers, artisans and artists, *macchiatino* is served in local *circoli* (social and recreation clubs) such as Volterra's Arci Garofano Rosso. If you'd like to blend in with locals, head to Caffè del Teatro at Via dei Sarti 40 and ask for a *macchiatino* at the aperitif hour.

The soft lighting and especially the white marble bar are the pride of owner Grazia. This is a classic old-fashioned Italian bar, one that has survived the recent hipster invasion unscathed and continues to attract a clientele of various ages and backgrounds. The warm, inviting atmosphere is accompanied by the carefully selected spirits resting atop the large coffee machine. And the small marble-topped tables are occupied by chatty pensioners, young folks reading the newspaper over their coffee, and grandmothers with their grandchildren enjoying an afternoon snack. The scene is a slice of life lost to many populations, but one that here in Volterra continues to withstand the changing times.

LIVORNO
The Free City

While touring Tuscany's markets, I would often approach the people behind the vegetable and fruit stands and shyly ask if I could take their photograph. At times they'd agree, but in most cases they would hide behind those enormous heads of lettuce and encourage me to shoot their hands only. Others would vanish entirely, taking their stories and recipes with them.

In Livorno, my experience was completely different. Here locals would practically chase me down or call me over to their stand: "What, you don't want to take my photo?" they'd ask.

I may be biased, but I've never had as much fun as I did at the Livorno market.

I got to know this city thanks to my best friend, Laura. Her grandmother, Rina, lived here, right next to the stadium, and during my early years at university we would spend weekends with her. I remember her tomato sauce, the pride in her eyes when she looked at her grandchildren, and her Sicilian-Livornese accent that would change based on whom she conversed with. As soon as we got there, Laura's mom would immediately take us to the fruit and vegetable market in Piazza Cavallotti, one of the liveliest markets I've ever seen, where we'd begin the day with fried *frati*, donut-like pastries that are simply unforgettable.

Livorno was a virtual assault of colors and aromas. I was equally struck by the uncommon congeniality and candor of its people and their symbiotic relationship with the sea. Today Livorno's Mascagni Terrace is still one of my favorite places in Tuscany: its hypnotic and beguiling checkerboard pavement draws you in and lures you towards the water.

Since then I've gone back often, having fallen for the local character and, naturally, the cuisine. "The Livornese cuisine is a feisty one, one of the common folk, but with that added zing of imagination." Who better to describe the food of this city than its own Aldo Santini?

The history of Livorno accounts for both the unique character of its people and its most renowned dishes. An "invented" city, Livorno was developed following Ferdinando I de' Medici's issuing of the Livorno Constitution in 1593, which granted various freedoms to anyone who moved there, including religious freedoms, freedom of dress and thought, and the right to organize initiatives and participate in political movements. As a result, Livorno quickly became one of the most important port cities in the Mediterranean, attracting people in search of easy earnings, along with businessmen, nobles and rich merchants. Racial diversity characterized the local population, including Livorno's wealthy classes, and this diversity and subsequent blending of cultures and traditions were to significantly influence the local cuisine.

The Central Food Market

WHERE: Via Buontalenti, Livorno.

WHEN: Every day from 6:30am to 1:30pm.

NOT TO MISS: Maruska's fish at the Mare Blu fish shop, the eggs at Parisi and the chickpea flour from Claudia and Raffaella Canovaro.

WHERE TO EAT: At Trattoria Antico Moro at Via Bartelloni 27, a rustic locale decorated with Chianti flasks and a bar counter papered with postcards. Try the *cacciucco* (fish stew) and the Livornese-style red mullet. Otherwise head to the La stuzzicheria di mare, located at Piazza Giuseppe Mazzini 66, a fish shop that doubles as restaurant.

WHERE TO STOP FOR A SNACK: Try the traditional cakes at Antica Torteria Al Mercato Da Gagarin at Via del Cardinale 24, just across from the market. Be sure to order the beverage called *spuma bionda* to accompany your snack.

OUTSIDE THE MARKET: Try the cakes at Sighieri as well, located at Via Ernesto Rossi 19.

Livorno's central food market, known to locals as the Mercato delle Vettovaglie, is located on the city's Scali Saffi along Reale Canal. Built at the end of the 19th century, this striking building features Neo-classical and Art Nouveau elements, influenced by European architecture at a time that favored the use of iron and glass. Today it's the second largest indoor market in Europe, second only to Barcelona's Boqueria.

The beating heart of the city, and still frequented daily by Livorno locals looking for fresh fish, meats, fruit and vegetables, this market boasts more than 180 stands offering everything you need from a market.
The strictly seasonal vegetables and fruit are grown in the surrounding countryside and are sold in the market's dedicated pavilion called Gabbrigiane, named for farmers from the village Gabbro, who would gather here every morning to sell their goods: chickens, eggs, rabbits and herbs. Bread, especially Tuscan bread, is well represented, coming from more than 10 different towns in the Livorno and Pisa areas.

The shops in the various pavilions along the market's edge offer every kind of spice and legume. Grains and flours are stored in enormous jute sacks. Naturally, chickpea flour is on hand here, being the main ingredient in Livorno's favorite snack and star of its street food scene.
Inside is a large area for meats: beef, pork and sheep products coming predominantly from nearby areas. You can also buy kosher meats here, evidence of the enduring influence of Jewish culture and cuisine on this city. The fun really starts at the lively fish market pavilion, the pride of every Livorno native, where sea aromas fill the air and the fish are so fresh they glitter as if still swimming in the waves of the Tyrrhenian sea.
The wide fish selection includes more economic types with lots of bones (good for soups), along with fish for frying, oily fish so plentiful in our nearby seas, more prized items such as shellfish and seafood, mounds of salted cod and rows of stock fish hung on the walls. Everything that ends up at one of these stands is the result of a delicate mix of factors: the luck and skill of the fishermen, the season, currents, and the weather, which whether forgiving or punishing is never predictable.

Piazza Cavallotti

WHERE: Piazza Cavallotti, Livorno.

WHEN: Every morning except Sundays.

NOT TO MISS: The fruit and vegetable stand run by Antonio, the "king of lettuce," and his vast range of fruit and vegetables.

WHERE TO EAT: At La Parmigiana, located at Piazza Luigi Orlando 8, for excellent fish and seafood dishes.

WHERE TO STOP FOR A SWEET SNACK: Try one (or more) of the lemon-scented *frati* at Antica Friggitoria at Via del Cardinale 9. Be warned: it's hard to stop with just one or two...

OUTSIDE THE MARKET: Complete your visit to Livorno with a glass of *ponce* (punch) at Civili at Via del Vigna 55.

Livorno is not what one would call a classically beautiful city. It possesses little of the brilliant Renaissance charm of Florence, or the elegance of Lucca, or the history-rich, red-bricked medieval palaces of Siena. Yet Livorno is beautiful—on its own terms, authentic terms. Here the villas and palaces range from Art Nouveau and Fascist-era styles to more modern buildings dating to the 1960s following the heavy bombing Livorno suffered during World War II.

Keep this in mind as you arrive in Piazza Cavallotti to visit the fruit and vegetable market. It will be nothing like the scene at Florence's Piazza Santo Spirito or Pistoia's Piazza della Sala. What you will see, however, is something genuinely and truly Livornese.

The stands line up along the vibrant colors of seasonal fruit and wooden crates full of fruits ripe and ready for making jams. The ground is covered with evidence of deals made and provisions obtained: leaves, peels and seeds.

Get in line and have a listen to the assured tone with which the women of Livorno conduct their shopping. Learn from their pairing ideas and their requests.

Then head to see Antonio, the "king of lettuce," and ask about ways to transform his vegetables into simple, genuine recipes. Pick up some red chili pepper, known in Tuscany and in Livorno by another name—*zenzero*, meaning "ginger", typically—as this is an often-mentioned ingredient in local recipes.

After visiting the market, you'll no doubt be ready for a Livornese breakfast, so head to the Antica Friggitoria, in business in this piazza since 1920. Here the most famous *frati* (donut-like pastries) in Livorno are made, those which generations of grandmothers have relied on to lift their grandchildren's spirits. Gobbled up in seconds, they then leave your lips dusted with sugar.

Ponce
Livornese

IL PONCE DEL CIVILI

Livornese Punch

You simply cannot leave Livorno without first stopping at Civili to experience the locals' favorite punch, or *ponce*. Civili is an old-school bar, full of tradition. Entering the small inconspicuous door, you find yourself in a low-lit scene replete with soccer pennants, old photographs and liquor bottles. The flooring is made of graniglia tiles, seen in homes in times past. In the veranda-covered garden, a few tables are set up here and there, surrounded by plastic chairs and friends come together for a chat and a glass of punch after lunch.

In the 1600s and 1700s, Livorno was one of the main ports in the Mediterranean, a multi-racial and international city of shipping agents and adventurers, bankers, merchants and diplomats. There were many English here at that time, often admired and emulated but with that touch of exuberant irony that still distinguishes the Livornese.
This is how English punch became Livorno *ponce*.

The British version starts with boiling water, lemon juice and Antilles rum—a spirit made with nutmeg and arak that was imported to England at the start of the 17th century by the East India Company. From there it spread throughout Europe. In Livornese *ponce*, the boiling water is replaced with a ristretto espresso, while the Antilles rum is substituted by a type called *fantasia*, a locally created spirit made with alcohol, sugar and dark caramel. These days some lemon zest is also added, but in the past a slice of lemon would have been inserted on the edge of the glass to create an extraordinary color contrast with the hot coffee. This version was called *ponce alla vela*.

So how does one make the real Livornese *ponce*? Start with a short, wide glass. Fill it halfway with coffee, then add the sugar (usually 2 tsp). Dissolve the sugar using the steam from the espresso machine, thus increasing the temperature of the coffee itself. Next fill the glass with rum and add the lemon zest.

This punch should be drunk hot, usually after lunch or dinner. It takes a bit getting used to, as the traditional *ponce* glass will be very hot indeed. Writer Aldo Santini offers these tips for drinking Livorno *ponce*:

Use three fingers of the right hand. The thumb and the middle finger to grip the thick base of the glass (the "butt," in other words), as this part of the glass will stay cool; and the index finger on the glass edge to balance and tilt it, so you're able to sip the right amount and enjoy it with a skilled slowness. Understood?
Aldo Santini, from *Il Ponce Livornese*, Edizioni Erasmo

MAREMMA

Maremma is likely one of Tuscany's wildest areas, along with Lunigiana, with which it shares the influences and feel of a border land—the first being very close to Lazio while the second lies between Liguria and Emilia.

Like many Tuscans, in my youth I spent several summers in Maremma. Summertime when you're young is about growing and exploring the world around you. Friendships are formed and sworn to last forever. Between the building of sand castles and learning how to swim with our heads underwater, memories are made that will last until adulthood and beyond.

Maremma was the backdrop of my summertime. After those initial long weeks spent in anticipation of the coming seaside holiday, I would finally be free to enjoy endless swims with my cousin and my sister, before the inevitable return to school.

Maremma often shows up in the colorful expressiveness of the Tuscan people, starting with the saying *Maremma cane* (a light curse meaning, literally, "Maremma dog") and on to increasingly imaginative epithets that only the Tuscan love of invective can generate. Formerly a swampy marshland, the Maremma area was considered unhealthy and dangerous, a place where one could easily die of disease, hunger or poverty.
During its malarial period, people would take refuge from the marshy plains high up in hilltop towns like Pitigliano, Sorano, Capalbio and Massa Marittima. Extensive redevelopment works later revitalized Maremma.

Abandoned for centuries, Maremma became a destination for seasonal workers from the Amiata, Casentino and Apennine mountains, who would descend from their mountainous homes to make charcoal. Maremma is also the land of buffalo and oxen cowboys known as *butteri*, the kind depicted by painters of the Macchiaioli movement and one of its founders, Giovanni Fattori. This is an unexpected, altogether wilder Tuscany, one very different from the stereotypical olive groves and vineyard-covered hills of Chianti.

More than markets, *sagre*, or food festivals, are common here. Held under huge white tents featuring long common tables, a *sagra* is the perfect place to try traditional dishes to counter seasonal temperatures, dishes like wild boar stew, pappardelle pasta with boar meat sauces, polenta with boar meat and other classics such as Maremma tortelli filled with ricotta and spinach.

Da MAURIZIO & SONIA
FRAGOLE
I^a COLTA
€8,00 AL KG

MELANZANE
€1,50
ALIFRUT

Orbetello, the Market by the Sea

WHERE: Via Caravaggio and Via Trento, Orbetello.

WHEN: Saturday mornings.

NOT TO MISS: The fish at Fratelli Canuzzi, both the fresh items and those pre-made, such as their paper-wrapped fish fry.

WHERE TO EAT: A truly memorable eating experience awaits you at the fishing cooperative I Pescatori, where the portions are plentiful, the fish the freshest available, and the dining right on the lagoon.

OUTSIDE THE MARKET: Head up Monte Argentario until you reach Ristoro La Sorgente, located along the provincial road 77 in a small hamlet called Convento, and have your fill of wild boar while you eat outside under the shade of pine trees.

My travels throughout Tuscany have led me to a wide variety of markets—bustling markets in neat, tree-lined piazzas, market stands scattered about tiny villages in places like Garfagnana and Lunigiana, grand indoor markets in Florence and Livorno, and lovely markets in deserted parking lots teeming with local products—but never before have I encountered a spectacle of this kind.

The Argentario promontory in southern Maremma is found just at the border with Lazio, along the Tuscan coast and the Orbetello lagoon. The city and its Saturday morning market are enveloped by the sea.

Market stands are lined up along the quay, providing shoppers with a background of sea blue and dazzling light dancing on the water's surface.

Fruit and vegetables here are all extremely fresh and locally sourced: light green zucchini with the flowers still on, watermelons stacked in enormous wooden crates, fragrant fish, local varieties of plums (small as olives and great for making jams), tiny eggplants to roast whole, and an extraordinary array of tomatoes in every shape and color.

Local cheeses are of course on hand as well, especially *pecorino*. Among the food stands, the one that attracts the most attention and longest lines is the Fratelli Canuzzi fish stand. Here you'll find two lines. On one side customers patiently await their turn to take home a tray of freshly fried fish with shrimps, cod and calamari—my favorites.

On the other side is the fresh fish, mostly local, from *moscardini*, or baby octopus, to *mostella*, a deep sea Mediterranean fish good for boiling, whose delicate meat is a hit with children.

After touring this market, you'll surely need a gelato break, so head to the *gelateria* Le Logge on Corso Italia to try their strictly seasonal, intensely flavored gelatos.

OFFERTA
PACCHI FAMIGLIA
CARNE MISTA
VITELLO

Grosseto, the Indoor Market

WHERE: Piazza dei Lavatoi, Grosseto.

WHEN: Monday through Saturday, though the best days are Thursday and Saturday.

NOT TO MISS: The meat from Enzo and Emilio's butcher shop, the fish from Fratelli Ciampoli, and the fresh fruit and vegetables from Stefano and Loretta.

WHERE TO HAVE BREAKFAST: At Crem café and pastry shop, located at Piazza Esperanto 4.

WHERE TO EAT: At Artidoro restaurant at Via de Barberi 12 near Grosseto's ancient city walls, or at the restaurant L'uva e il Malto at Via Giuseppe Mazzini 165 to try their meat, game, fish soups.

Grosseto's indoor market is a symbolic representation of the two sides of the Maremma: the inland, comprised of woods, hunting, game, meats, mushrooms and soups; and the coastal, distinguished by ripe fruit and vegetables, sea and fish.

This market is not as grand as those in Livorno or Florence. It is more modest, and in this aspect truly reflects the Maremma character.

Its historic stands bring together all the wonderful products of Maremma in one small space, in particular meat, fish and vegetables. The Porto Santo Stefano fish stand is especially good. Ask for Fabio, who gives the best advice on how to choose the right fish for any dish and how to cook every kind of local fish imaginable.

In the center of the market is Stefano and Loretta's stand, looking like a Flemish painting of fruit and vegetables, among which are the sweetest seasonal strawberries, bunches of artichokes and other Maremma specialties. Once again, the aromas of my summers spent at the seaside come back to me.

Just across from the market is Crem café and pastry shop, where you'll find artisanal pastries, desserts, and soft, wonderful slow-leavened croissants to pair with a coffee or cappuccino.

Capalbio, the Smaller Markets

WHERE: Along Maremma's inland and coastal roads.

WHEN: Spring and summer (when the weather is good).

NOT TO MISS: The locally grown fruit and vegetables, and the bunches of fresh basil the size of wedding bouquets.

WHERE TO EAT: Try Rosso e Vino alla Dogana on Via Graticciaia, Chiarone Scalo, for Tuscan seafood to enjoy right on the beach.

OUTSIDE THE MARKET: Head to the beach resort Ultima Spiaggia for a glorious seaside day of crystalline waters and soft, white sand. The beach extends out to the Lago di Burano natural oasis.

When we used to take trips to the Maremma seaside, we never stopped to buy fruit and vegetables at the supermarket, nor at the regular markets. Instead, our points of reference were the farmers' stands that would appear suddenly around bends in the road or at roadside stopping points, protected from the ferocious summer sun by reed screening or the shade of gracious pine trees.
We'd pile the shopping onto our bicycles and head back, loaded down with fish and eggplants arranged in a way to keep us from losing our balance.

The intensely sweet fruit scents I encountered there were the aromatic draw of my loveliest summers. Later I would encounter that smell in wintertime, in the jams my mother used to make at home for spreading on bread as a snack or to bake in Sunday tarts.

When I got to the Capalbio area in search of markets, the most picturesque and genuine things I came across were the endlessly fascinating fruit and vegetable stands. Drive slowly through the region. You will soon see one of these countless local stands suddenly appear on the horizon, often marked by hand-written signs praising the quality of produce. It was while driving along the Aurelia road that we happened upon Gianni's stand, at the turnoff to Capalbio Scalo.

In summertime, he sells everything grown in his fields and fruit orchards here at his stand: tomatoes, cucumbers, peaches, watermelons and other types of melon, enormous bunches of basil, and occasionally olive oil, wine, jams and preserves.

I asked Gianni for some tips on how to make the dish *acquacotta* (literally, "cooked water"), and what followed was one of the most extraordinary things to happen during my travels around Tuscany's markets.

Saying that he had no idea how to make the dish, he asked me to follow him, as he knew just the right person to help me. I nearly ran to keep up with him as we traversed a sun-scorched field and ended up knocking on the door of the house belonging to Ilena, a retired cook who opened her home to us. I sat down in her tidy, cool, dimly lit living room, where I proceeded to jot down notes, amazed by the generosity before me.

Vendita Diretta
di
Ortaggi e
frutta

BREAD

PANE SCIOCCO
Unsalted Bread

You can't talk about Tuscan cuisine without mentioning *pane sciocco*, or unsalted bread. It has a crunchy crust, slightly golden color and a soft, dense inside.

It takes a while to get used to, but for those accustomed to it from birth, who since nursery school have been served an afternoon snack with prosciutto, tomato, jam, or simply oil and salt—this is bread.

The reasons for its being made without salt at times border on legend: one version points to the high tax Pisa placed on salt, to which Florentines responded by starting to make bread without it. But perhaps there's a simpler explanation. If you've ever tasted a well-cured prosciutto crudo or aged pecorino cheese, you'll have noticed that these items need a bread that can balance out intense saltiness.

That's why the first recipe in this Tuscan cookbook is one for unsalted bread. Others will follow, of course, such as Lunigiana chestnut flour bread and potato bread from Garfagnana, but this bread is the most important. It helps us to understand the Tuscan character and the character of our cooking. What's more, it allows us, when turning to the pages where pappa al pomodoro and panzanella are found, to successfully recreate these recipes, having all the ingredients at hand—including this most important one.

PANE TOSCANO

Tuscan Bread

from Sant'Ambrogio Market in Florence

Tuscan bread is made from a few essential ingredients: flour, yeast, and water. A strong flour is needed for the biga, a pre-ferment commonly used in Italian baking that must ripen for about twenty hours to give the bread the aroma that makes it so special. For the bread dough, on the other hand, a weaker flour is used to give the loaf its characteristic texture, crunchy crust and rather dense inside.

When this bread turns stale, it will be soaked in water and used to make *panzanella* or *pappa al pomodoro*, and it's the weaker flour used in the dough that allows the bread to come back to life, to be softened and then crumbled into a large heap.

INGREDIENTS FOR 4 PEOPLE

FOR THE BIGA

300 g (2 & 1/4 cups) strong flour
150 g (2/3 cup) water, room temperature
4 g (about 1/4 of a 0.6-oz cake) fresh baker's yeast

FOR THE DOUGH

biga made prior
1 kg (8 cups) all-purpose flour
600 ml (2 & 1/2 cups) tepid water
2 g (about 1/8 of a 0.6-oz cake) fresh yeast (optional)
extra virgin olive oil

Make the biga the day before. In a medium-sized bowl, dissolve the yeast in the room temperature water and add the flour. Briskly mix the ingredients until combined, then cover the bowl with plastic wrap. Let the dough ripen at room temperature for 20 to 24 hours. For the dough, start by dissolving the yeast in half the water.

If you have time, you can leave out the yeast and instead extend the rising time.

Combine the biga, flour, water, and yeast in a stand mixer bowl. Knead with the dough hook on high and gradually add the rest of the water, continuing until a smooth, uniform, elastic dough forms. Do not knead for more than 15 minutes.

Let the dough rest for about a half hour in a bowl greased with olive oil, then divide the dough into 4 parts of 500 g each.

Form each portion of dough into a loaf, keeping the ends slightly narrower. Transfer the loaves to a well-floured tea towel, with the towel closed on the underside, and let rest at room temperature, away from drafts. Let the loaves double in size.

Heat the oven to 200°C/400°F. Gently turn out the loaves onto

a baking sheet covered with baking paper or onto a baking stone. Bake for around 45 minutes or until the loaves are golden and make a hollow sound when tapped on the bottom.

PAN DI RAMERINO

Rosemary Bread

from Sant'Ambrogio Market in Florence

In Florence it's long been a tradition to make rosemary bread buns on Good Friday, which is then taken to mass to be blessed. Today this traditional Easter dessert is found throughout the year at Florentine bakeries, including those at the Sant'Ambrogio and San Lorenzo markets. At Sant'Ambrogio stop by Panrocco, where together with rosemary bread buns you'll find castagnaccio (a specialty cake made with chestnut flour), olive oil schiacciata, coccoli (fried balls of bread dough), and all kinds of baked goods typically found at a Florentine bakery. The flavor of this bread is similar to other traditional Tuscan leavened cakes, in which rosemary, oil, and raisins are used to transform an otherwise simple bread dough into something special for holidays or other important moments in the year. Consider the Sienese *pan co' santi* (literally, "bread with saints") typically prepared for All Souls' Day, or the grape schiacciata made during the harvest.

INGREDIENTS FOR 20 BUNS

FOR THE BIGA
2 g (about 1/8 of a 0.6-oz cake) fresh yeast
75 g (1/3 cup) water, room temperature
150 g (1 & 1/8 cups) bread flour

FOR THE ROSEMARY BREAD DOUGH
biga made prior
2 g (about 1/8 of a 0.6-oz cake) fresh yeast
500 g (4 cups) medium-strong flour
70 g (1/3 cup) brown sugar
250 ml (1 cup) tepid water
10 g (1/2 tbsp) salt
120 g (1/2 cup) extra virgin olive oil
200 g (1 & 1/3 cups) raisins
1 small glass vinsanto
8 g (1/4 oz) rosemary sprigs
1 egg for the glaze

FOR THE SUGAR SYRUP
100 ml (1/2 cup) water
100 g (1/2 cup) sugar
1/2 vanilla pod

Make the biga the day before. In a medium-sized bowl, dissolve the yeast in the room temperature water and add the flour. Briskly mix the ingredients until combined, then cover the bowl with plastic wrap and let it ripen at room temperature for 20 to 24 hours.

Make the buns. Soak the raisins in the vinsanto and a small amount of water, enough to cover them, for about an hour, then drain and squeeze out the excess liquid.

Chop the rosemary very finely and transfer to a pan with the olive oil. Heat the oil and rosemary on low and remove the pan from the heat as soon as the herbs start to brown.

Let the oil mixture cool to room temperature.

Dissolve the yeast in half of the warm water.

Combine the biga, flour and sugar in a stand mixer and knead well using the bread hook for 5 minutes.

Add the salt and continue mixing, adding the water a small amount at a time until the dough is smooth, firm, and just starting to pull away from sides of the bowl.

You can also knead the dough by hand, a long process requiring patience but doable.

CONTINUED ON PAGE 135

CONTINUATION OF PAGE 132

Next add the oil and rosemary and continue kneading with the bread hook on low for about 10 minutes, until the dough has absorbed all the oil and become smooth but not too sticky and pulls away from the hook. In the last 5 minutes, add the raisins and mix long enough to incorporate them.

Transfer the dough to a bowl greased with olive oil. Let rest for about 15 minutes in a warm area, such as inside a closed oven with the light turned on.

After the dough has rested, divide it into equal pieces weighing

60 g each. Next form the round buns. This step is not difficult, but it does require some practice. Using both hands, fold the dough onto itself so that each piece forms a tight ball.

Transfer them to two baking sheets lined with baking paper, making sure to leave a good amount of space between them as they will enlarge during cooking.

Beat the egg together with a spoonful of water and carefully brush each bun. Let the buns rise for about 25 minutes. Cross the buns with two vertical and two horizontal slices across the surface of each, pressing firmly, then repeat the glaze and let them rise again. They should double in size.

Heat the oven to 180°C/350°F and cook the buns for about 15 to 20 minutes or until they are golden and puffed.

Meanwhile, make the syrup by boiling the sugar and water together with the opened vanilla pod for about 10 minutes.

Remove the buns when cooked and brush them with the syrup while still hot, then sprinkle them with small sprigs of rosemary.

Let cool. They are best served still slightly warm, but they keep well for 5 to 6 days in a cookie tin or ziplock plastic bag.

SCHIACCIATA ALL'OLIO

Tuscan Flatbread with Olive Oil

from Colle Val d'Elsa Market

In every market there's at least one stand that sells salami and other cured meats, sandwiches and *schiacciata*. Tuscan *schiacciata* has almost a cult following. There are those who prefer it soft and slightly oily, while for others there's never enough olive oil. Some want it thin and crunchy. Some want it cooked on a baking stone. And then there are those who simply cannot help themselves whenever it's around. With one bite of *schiacciata*, many a Tuscany native is transported back to childhood and school snack time.

INGREDIENTS FOR 2 BAKING PANS MEASURING 33 X 25 CM (13 X 10 INCHES)

FOR THE POOLISH

1 g (about 1/16 of a 0.6-oz cake) fresh yeast
250 g (1 & 3/4 cups) bread flour
250 g (1 cup) cold water

FOR THE DOUGH

poolish made prior
500 g (4 cups) all-purpose flour
250 g (1 cup) slightly lukewarm water
1 tsp salt
1 tsp honey
2 tbsp extra virgin olive oil, plus more for greasing the pans

Make the poolish the day before. I suggest making it around dinner time, as it requires at least 12 hours of ripening. Dissolve the yeast in cold water in a large bowl, then add the strong flour and whisk to remove any clumps. Cover the bowl with plastic wrap and let rest at room temperature until the next day. After 12 hours the poolish will be ready. It should be active and bubbling.

To make the dough, place the poolish in a large bowl. Add the flour, salt, honey and olive oil. Gradually add in the lukewarm water. Knead on a pastry board (or inside the bowl itself) for about 10 minutes, enough for the dough to absorb the water as you add it in a little at a time.

Lightly oil your hands and form a ball with the dough. Oil the bowl and place the dough inside. Cover with plastic wrap and let ripen at room temperature until the dough has doubled in size, at least 3 hours.

When the dough has risen, oil your hands again and gently deflate it. Divide into two equal parts. Oil the two baking pans. Slowly roll the dough out directly in each pan: press the dough outwards with your hands, letting it relax a bit after each pressing. Then leave to rest in the baking pans. Over the next two hours, continue to gently press the dough out with oiled hands until it completely covers the pan.

Heat the oven to 220°C/430°F. Oil the surface of the schiacciata and dust with coarse salt. Bake for at least 20 to 25 minutes, until the bread is puffed and golden.

PAN CO' SANTI

"Bread with Saints"

from the Farmers Market in Siena

In Siena, you can always tell the time of year based on the types of sweets available at any given moment. In September, a few spoonfuls of sugar and grapes are added to plain bread dough to make a *schiacciata* traditionally associated with the harvest. Late October to mid-November, on the other hand, means the arrival of *pan co' santi*, a Tuscan sweet bread made with sugar, raisins and walnuts. Its name derives from an association with All Saints' Day on November 1. Pan co' santi will be followed later by Christmastime treats like *cavallucci*, *panforte* and *ricciarelli*.

INGREDIENTS FOR 2 LOAVES

FOR THE POOLISH
200 g (1 & ⅔ cups) bread flour
200 g (¾ cup) water
1 g (about 1⁄16 of a 0.6-oz cake) yeast

FOR THE DOUGH
poolish made prior
250 g (1 & ¾ cups) raisins
100 g (½ cup) extra virgin olive oil
300 g (10 & ½ oz) shelled walnuts
50 g (¼ cup) sugar
50 g (¼ cup) lukewarm water
5 g (⅓ of a 0.6 oz cake) fresh yeast
600 g (4 & ¾ cups) all-purpose flour
150 ml (⅔ cup) red wine
1 tsp salt
½ tsp pepper
1 egg yolk for the glaze

Make the poolish the day before, preferably in the evening.

Dissolve the yeast in the water and mix in the flour. You should have a smooth and fairly liquid mixture. Cover with plastic wrap and let rest for 10 to 12 hours.

For the dough, start by soaking the raisins in a bowl of water.

Heat the olive oil in a pan. Chop the walnuts and drain and dry the raisins. Add both to the pan with the sugar.

Let the oil take on flavor and then remove from the heat and let cool.

Dissolve the yeast in lukewarm water. Add this to the poolish along with the flour and the nut and raisin oil. Knead in a stand mixer bowl on low speed, adding the wine a little at a time, until the dough is well combined. It should be smooth to the touch and come away easily from your hands. Lastly, add the salt and pepper and knead for another minute.

Turn the dough out onto an oiled pastry board. Form a round ball of the dough and let rise for about 2 hours, until doubled in size.

When the dough has doubled in size, knead it again, then divide and form 2 loaves. Cross the tops of each with a knife and let rise again until doubled in size.

Next glaze them with the beaten egg yolk and bake at 180°C/350°F for about 40 minutes. Let the bread cool thoroughly. Wait at least one day before consuming.

Store wrapped in a tea towel or a paper bag.

IL PANE DI MAROCCA DI CASOLA

Marocca di Casola Bread

Finding a quality chestnut flour these days can be a challenge, and an expensive one.
Yet chestnut flour is a cardinal ingredient in Tuscany's peasant and mountain cooking traditions, from Garfagnana and the Pistoiese Mountains to the Mugello and Mount Amiata regions.
During lean times when supplies were hard to come by, the versatile and highly caloric chestnut nourished local populations.

The flour made from chestnuts is used in polenta, bread, cakes, cookies, fresh pasta and *necci*.
Chestnuts require milling, such as that carried out by the Antico Mulino Rossi mill in Fivizzano since 1898.
For over a hundred years, this mill has been the local go-to for grinding grains and chestnuts in the traditional method: a large stone grinder.

It was here at this mill that I met Mariangela, a woman as strong and as sweet as the chestnut flour wafting through the air. She spoke to me about chestnut flour's fundamental role in traditional Lunigiana cooking, in dishes like gnocchi, *castagnaccio*, fritters and the dark bread known as *marocca*.
Today *Marocca di Casola* bread is a Slow Food presidium, produced in Regnano at Fabio Bertolucci's bakery in Canoàra. It's a dense, spongy bread that goes well with ricotta and chestnut honey, anchovies, lardo di Colonnata and local pancetta.

MAROCCA

Chestnut Flour Bread

from Fivizzano's Market

INGREDIENTS FOR 2 LOAVES

FOR THE BIGA
2 g (1/8 of a 0.6 oz cake) fresh yeast
100 g (1/2 cup) cold water
200 g (1 & 2/3 cups) all-purpose flour

FOR THE DOUGH
biga made prior
5 g (1/3 of a 0.6 oz cake) fresh yeast (optional)
400 g (3 & 1/3 cups) soft wheat flour, medium strength
300 g (2 & 1/3 cups) chestnut flour
200 g (2/3 cup) boiled potato, mashed
200 g (3/4 cup) water, room temperature
15 g (2 & 1/2 tsp) salt
corn flour
olive oil

Make the biga the day before by dissolving the yeast in cold water in a medium bowl. Add the flour. Briskly mix the ingredients until thoroughly combined, then cover the bowl with plastic wrap. Let the dough ripen overnight at room temperature.

For the dough, start by boiling the potatoes whole (so they absorb less water). Peel them and mash with a potato masher to avoid lumps.

Dissolve the yeast in half of the lukewarm water. If you have time, you can leave out the yeast and instead extend the rising time.

In a stand mixer bowl, combine the biga, the two flours, the potato mash, and the water and yeast.

Knead with the dough hook on high and gradually add the rest of the water and salt, continuing until a smooth, uniform, elastic dough forms.

Do not knead for more than 10 minutes.

Let the dough rest for about 30 minutes in a bowl greased with olive oil, then divide the dough into 2 parts.

Form each portion of dough into a loaf by rolling the dough onto itself, keeping the ends slightly narrower. Let ripen at room temperature on a surface dusted with corn flour, protected from drafts. Dust the outside of the loaves with corn flour.

The loaves should double in size.

Heat the oven to 220°C/425°F. Gently turn out the loaves onto a baking sheet covered with baking paper or onto a baking stone. Bake for around 30 minutes, then lower the heat to 180°C/350°F and bake for another 30 minutes, until the loaves are golden and make a hollow sound when tapped on the bottom.

PANE DI PATATE

Potato Bread

from Castelnuovo di Garfagnana's Market

INGREDIENTS FOR 2 LOAVES

FOR THE BIGA
2 g (1/8 of a 0.6 oz cake) fresh yeast
150 g (2/3 cup) water, room temperature
300 g (2 & 1/2 cups) all-purpose flour

FOR THE DOUGH
biga made prior
5 g (1/3 of a 0.6 oz cake) fresh yeast (optional)
450 g (1 lb) soft wheat flour, medium strength
50 g (1/3 cup) semolina flour
250 g (1/2 lb) potatoes, boiled and mashed
150 g (2/3 cup) water, room temperature
15 g (2 & 1/2 tsp) salt
corn flour

Make the biga the day before by dissolving the yeast in the room temperature water in a medium bowl. Add the flour. Briskly mix the ingredients until thoroughly combined, then cover the bowl with plastic wrap. Let the biga ripen overnight at room temperature.

Make the dough. Start by boiling the unpeeled, whole potatoes (they will absorb less water). They are ready when a knife pierces them easily. Drain, peel and mash with potato masher to avoid any lumps.

Dissolve the yeast in half of the lukewarm water. If you have time, you can skip the yeast and instead extend the rising time.

In a stand mixer bowl, combine the biga, the two flours, the potato mash and the water and yeast mixture. Knead with the dough hook on high. Gradually add the rest of the water and the salt, continuing until a smooth, uniform, elastic dough forms.
Do not knead for more than 10 minutes.

Let the dough rest for about a half hour in a bowl greased with olive oil, then divide the dough into 2 parts.

Form each portion of dough into a loaf by rolling it onto itself, keeping the ends slightly narrower. Dust with the corn flour and let rise at room temperature on a work surface or table dusted with plenty of corn flour, away from drafts. The loaves should double in size.

Heat the oven to 220°C/430°F. Gently turn out the loaves onto a baking sheet covered with baking paper or onto a baking stone. Bake for around 25 minutes, then lower the heat to 180°C/350°F and bake for another 30 minutes, until the loaves are golden and make a hollow sound when tapped on the bottom.

APPETIZERS

PANZANELLA RICCA COL TONNO

Panzanella with Tuna

from Colle Val d'Elsa Market

Panzanella is made in layers. The base ingredient is unsalted Tuscan bread that has gone stale by a few days, which is then soaked in water, wrung out and combined with tomato, cucumber, onion, oil, salt, red wine vinegar and basil. As often happens, however, every cook ends up creating a version wholly theirs, by adding or leaving out ingredients according to individual preference. Known since Boccaccio's time as "washed bread," this ancient recipe was later immortalized by Renaissance painter and poet Bronzino (1503-1572), who wrote of a green panzanella made with onion, cucumber, purslane and arugula. Tomatoes were not included, as they had just been introduced to Europe from the Americas and were not yet commonplace. At my house we make the classic panzanella, without exception. But then friends arrive, each wanting a different version. Some want a panzanella without onion, others prefer it without cucumber. Then there are those who, like my husband Tommaso, love it with tuna and capers. Panzanella is one of those dishes that invariably bends to the mood of the day and what's on hand in the garden or pantry.

INGREDIENTS FOR 4 PEOPLE

300 g (10 & ½ oz) stale Tuscan bread (a few days old)
160 g (5 & ½ oz) oil-packed tuna
1 Certaldo onion (or other sweet red onion variety)
2 tomatoes, either Florentine Costoluti or Beefsteak variety
1 cucumber
about 10 basil leaves
salt
freshly ground black pepper
extra virgin olive oil
red wine vinegar or apple cider vinegar

Break up the bread and place the pieces in a large bowl. Cover with cold water.

Finely slice the onion. The Certaldo onion is a sweet variety, but if the flavor of your onions is too strong, soak them in cold water for about 10 minutes to reduce their pungency.

Roughly chop the tomatoes. Peel and finely slice the cucumber.

Drain and wring out the bread to remove all excess liquid, then crumble it using your hands. There's nothing worse than a too-watery panzanella, so just when you think you have wrung out the liquid sufficiently, go ahead and do it one more time.

Transfer the crumbled bread to a large bowl such as a soup tureen. Drain the tuna and the onions (if applicable) and add these to the bread along with the tomatoes and the cucumber. Tear in the basil leaves in the bowl.

Season with salt, pepper, plenty of extra virgin olive oil and a small amount of red wine vinegar. For a more delicate flavor, use apple cider vinegar. Refrigerate for at least 30 minutes, then toss well and serve.

CIPOLLE DOLCI DI CERTALDO
Sweet Certaldo Onions

My friend Judy, an American chef and cooking teacher, recommended I seek out Erica in Certaldo, an ever-reliable source when it comes to onions.
Erica works for the D'Ercole family farm, which delivers organic, authentic seasonal products to the Certaldo market and other towns near Florence.
Their products exemplify everything we like to see at a farmers market: fruits and vegetables left to ripen naturally, grains, dried legumes, jams and extra virgin olive oil.
Talking about Certaldo onions always leads one back to Boccaccio, on account of a story in *The Decameron* dedicated to a friar who goes by the name Fra Cipolla (*cipolla* means "onion" in Italian).

Certaldo, as you may have heard, is a burgh of Val d'Elsa situated in our country, which, small though it be, was once inhabited by gentlemen and men of substance; and thither, for that he found good pasture there, one of the friars of the order of St. Anthony was long used to resort once a year, to get in the alms bestowed by simpletons upon him and his brethren. His name was Fra Cipolla and he was gladly seen there, no less belike, for his name's sake than for other reasons, seeing that these parts produce onions that are famous throughout all Tuscany.

Giovanni Boccaccio, *The Decameron*

Onions have long been part of local identity, in short. During the 12th century they were even featured on a feudal coat-of-arms, a symbol of this peasant culture with ancient origins.
This is my grandmother's favorite onion, the one she gladly uses in her panzanella, boiled beef and soups, given its sweetness. For me, when summer arrives Certaldo onions mean making jam, which is the best way to preserve them in winter and the perfect accompaniment to local pecorino cheeses.

CIPOLLE AL FORNO CON PANE, PECORINO E CAPPERI

Baked Onions with Bread, Pecorino and Capers

from Certaldo's Market

Years ago in Certaldo I met Gabriele. He used to sell bread and cheese there. Always smiling, he would call you over to taste a slice of his goat's milk grana cheese or a little piece of bread with oil. Behind his decision to set up a market business with his daughter Carlotta is a story of solidarity, one that will have you stopping to smile with him.

He knows which cheese to recommend for every occasion and for every recipe. When I told him I wanted to make baked onions, he expertly cut me a slice of Sienese pecorino, because, as he explained, it melts without releasing liquid and is thus best suited to baked dishes.

INGREDIENTS FOR 4 PEOPLE

3 medium Certaldo onions (or other sweet red onion)
2 slices stale Tuscan bread
80 g (3 oz) medium-aged Sienese pecorino cheese
1 small bunch fresh parsley
1 garlic clove
1 tbsp salt-packed capers
1 tbsp pitted black olives
salt
freshly ground black pepper
extra virgin olive oil

Peel the onions and remove the outer layer. Slice them length-wise to about 1 cm (½ inch) thickness. Cover a baking sheet with baking paper. Grease with olive oil and arrange the onions on top, with the slices side by side.

Make the dressing. Briefly soak the stale bread in cold water. Finely chop the parsley with the garlic, the rinsed capers and the pitted olives. Drain the bread and squeeze the excess liquid from it. Add the mince of capers, parsley, garlic and olives. Add the grated pecorino and adjust for salt and pepper.

Sprinkle the dressing mixture on the onion slices and finish by drizzling with olive oil. Using softened stale bread rather than bread crumbs allows the onions to cook without becoming too dry.

Heat the oven to 200°C/390°F. Bake the onions for about 45 minutes, until they are soft and golden. Serve as an hors d'oeuvres, like canapes.

TONNO DEL CHIANTI

Chianti "Tuna"

from Greve in Chianti Market

This fairly recent recipe, rediscovered and made famous by Dario Cecchini, the "butcher poet" of Panzano in Chianti, calls for a leg of pork. In recreating it at home I ended up using a pork loin rather than a ham, since that's what I had on hand. Then, while researching the origins of this recipe and other ways to prepare it, I came across a version by Paolo Petroni, who suggests using lean pork loin or tenderloin. It is similar to the rabbit "tuna" of Piedmont, very simple and requiring only a bit of planning and patience.
Start a few days in advance by removing the fat from the loin, salting it and leaving it in the refrigerator to expel excess liquids. The cooking will be slow on low heat. Once the meat is cooked and flavored, you will have to wait a few weeks more (or better still, a month) to allow the flavors to set and the meat to transform into a true Chianti "tuna."

INGREDIENTS FOR 4 PEOPLE

800 g (1 & ¾ lb) pork loin
coarse salt
1 l (4 & ¼ cups) dry white wine
4 bay leaves
2 tbsp black peppercorns
2 tbsp juniper berries
extra virgin olive oil

Using a very sharp knife, remove the excess fat from the loin. Then cut the meat into 4 or 5 pieces and place inside a bowl. Cover with a few handfuls of coarse salt then close with a sheet of aluminum foil. Let rest in the fridge for 3 days.

After 3 days, rinse the meat under running water to remove the excess salt, transfer it to a pot, cover it with the wine and add 2 of the bay leaves. Lightly crush a tablespoon each of black peppercorns and juniper berries and add to the pot.

Put the pot on the lowest heat, cover and cook the meat for about 3 hours, maintaining a very low boil. When the pork loin is well done, remove it from the heat and let cool completely.

Drain the meat and let dry on paper towels for an hour. Break the meat up with a fork and transfer to a glass jar, adding the remaining bay leaves, black pepper and juniper.

Press the meat down well to remove any bubbles, then cover with extra virgin olive oil. Store in the refrigerator for a month before using.

Remove the Chianti "tuna" from the fridge a few hours before serving to bring to room temperature. Serve as an appetizer or main course along with boiled beans and finely chopped fresh red onion.

CROSTINI DI FEGATINI DI POLLO E CONIGLIO

Crostini with Chicken and Rabbit Liver Pâté

from the Farmers Market in Siena

At any meat counter or butcher shop at the local market, always let your senses guide you, but be sure to follow along with the friendly chit chat as well. I don't know about you, but I have always been lucky in finding jovial and chatty butchers, who not only sell you quality meat but also give you cooking ideas: on how to use economic cuts, or how to impress your mother-in-law with something as simple as *fettina alla pizzaiola,* a cut of steak cooked "in the style of a pizza," meaning with tomato and herbs.
Listen in as butchers chat with the women in line, as they can't help but talk about their own recipes, about how they roast certain meats or how wonderful their rabbit liver pâté is—a Sunday tradition and a recipe they don't share with just anyone.

INGREDIENTS FOR 4 PEOPLE

- 2 carrots
- 1 celery stalk
- 1 small white onion
- 1 shallot
- 1 small bunch fresh parsley
- extra virgin olive oil
- 700 g (1 & ½ lb) chicken livers and hearts
- 300 g (⅔ lb) rabbit livers
- 200 ml (¾ cup) light vegetable broth
- 1 tbsp salt-packed capers, rinsed and dried
- anchovy paste

Make a mince of celery, onion, carrots, parsley and shallot.
Cover the bottom of a medium-sized heavy pot with olive oil and add the mince.
Cook on medium heat for about 5 minutes, then add all the livers and chicken hearts. Stir with a wooden spoon and brown the organs well. When they start to lighten in color, losing their redness and turning brown, add the broth and cook for about 10 minutes.
At the end of the cooking time, add the rinsed capers.

Next consider what kind of texture you would like to obtain for the pâté. Chop the organ meats, and to render the pâté even creamier, process through a food mill for a smooth yet rustic texture. Alternatively, process with an immersion blender to obtain a true creamy pâté. I like a more rustic pâté, so I usually process only about half with the food mill or blender.

Now transfer the pâté back to the pot and cook on low heat. Add the anchovy paste, which lends a perfect saltiness. Cook for 1 minute. The pâté is now ready.

Store the pâté in the fridge for a few days. Heat it up slightly before serving on small pieces of sliced bread. An alternative way to serve is to first butter the bread slices or dip them in broth. Otherwise, serve simply by spreading on toasted bread.

COCCINI DI PANE E PECORINO

Bread and Pecorino Cheese en Cocotte

from Pienza's Market

This recipe for pecorino *coccini* (Italian for *en cocotte*) is from Luisa, the cook with the welcoming smile at Agriturismo Il Rigo between Pienza and San Quirico d'Orcia.
To judge this starter dish by reading the ingredients alone, you would never guess how special it is. Once you have tasted it, however, I guarantee it will become an instant classic at your dinner parties with friends.

INGREDIENTS FOR 4 PEOPLE

extra virgin olive oil
12 slices bread (1-2 days old)
240 g (8 & ½ oz) soft pecorino cheese
white wine such as Vernaccia
truffle butter

Heat the oven to 180°C/350°F.

Oil 4 oven proof earthenware cocotte dishes.

Slice the bread into 12 slices about 1 cm thick (0.5 inch) so that they fit perfectly into the cocottes. Slice the cheese into 12 slices about 5 mm thick.

Layer in the bread and cheese, alternating, starting with a slice of bread and finishing with a slice of cheese. Moisten each layer with a bit of wine. Finish with a teaspoon of the truffle butter.

Cook in the oven for 15 minutes and serve immediately.

BARBOTLA CON FIORI DI ZUCCA

Barbotla with Zucchini Flowers

from Pontremoli's Market

We pedaled under the early summer sun in the Lunigiana hills, passing quasi-abandoned hamlets and lively and picturesque towns like Pontremoli. We sought the shade of trees the way a parched man searches for a desert oasis, anticipating with ever-increasing faith the end of that climb. We had a purpose, and the kilometers progressed quickly as we flew past the roadside landscapes. Once we'd arrived at the Saudon holiday farm, we looked out onto the world below. Our goal that day had been lunch outdoors under a veranda overlooking the Lunigiana valleys—a lunch comprised of local, traditional foods cooked in *testi di ghisa,* large cast iron pots characteristic of this region. Starter dishes began arriving as soon as we sat down. Along with them, a thin *schiacciata* bread similar to *cecina,* a pancake-like specialty made from chickpea flour, but with a different texture and the unique flavor of zucchini flowers. This is *barbotla,* similar to a thin focaccia but with the addition of zucchini flowers. A specialty of Lunigiana, it is served as a starter dish or as a unique addition to an Italian aperitivo, either on its own or accompanied by some slices of cured meats. If you happen to visit a market during the brief period in which zucchini flowers are radiating their bright, sunny yellow among the vegetable stands, treat yourself to a bunch and make this dish. Lacking zucchini flowers, you can use a tender zucchini. If, on the other hand, you are one of the lucky ones who either have a garden of your own or are blessed by generous gardening neighbors, use a quantity of flowers equal to the weight of one zucchini. Do not forget the basil: it adds a special fragrance.

INGREDIENTS FOR 8 PEOPLE

200 g (7 oz) zucchini flowers
350 g (2 & ¾ cups) all-purpose flour
50 g (½ cup) corn flour
550 ml (1 cup) cold water
3 tbsp extra virgin olive oil, plus more for greasing the pan
about 10 basil leaves
15 g (3 tsp) salt
freshly ground black pepper

Heat the oven to 250°/475°F and place a 11 x 15 inch/28 x 38 cm baking sheet in it.

Clean the zucchini flowers and remove the pistils, then cut them into thin strips. Set them aside.

Mix the all-purpose flour and corn flour with cold water. Tear the basil leaves into pieces and add them to the flour along with the oil, salt, and pepper. Transfer to the fridge.

When the oven is hot, remove the baking sheet, grease with olive oil and add the batter, making sure to level it. Evenly distribute the zucchini flowers on top of the batter, pressing them down to submerge them. Drizzle some more oil on the top.

Reduce the temperature to 200°C/400°F and transfer the baking sheet into the oven. Bake for 45 to 50 minutes, until the surface is golden and crunchy.

Serve hot, dusted with pepper, on its own or alongside cured meats and cheeses, and enjoy its lovely summertime fragrance.

SALSA ROSSA ALL'ALLORO

Red Sauce with Bay Leaves

from Castelnuovo di Garfagnana's Market

Just outside the town walls and near Castelnuovo di Garfagnana's cathedral you can find a quaint *osteria,* Il Vecchio Mulino. Part bar, part enoteca, and a bit of an old-fashioned food shop, this *osteria* doesn't offer cooked dishes, but instead an array of excellent products exemplifying the true food and wine traditions of Garfagnana. Launched in the early 1900s, today Il Vecchio Mulino still has the feel of an old-fashioned rest stop. Cheeses and cured meats are served with potato bread, savory rice tarts, pecorino and potatoes, spelt salad, chestnut flour desserts and spelt amber beer. The place has everything!
This red sauce recipe comes from Il Vecchio Mulino. In Garfagnana, it's always made for festivities like birthdays, baptisms and weddings. The anchovy paste and capers work with the sweetness of the tomato and the bite of the vinegar to create a perfect balance of flavors. Serve it with the potato bread on page 144, but be sure to make enough, as it is nearly impossible to stop at one taste.

INGREDIENTS FOR 4 PEOPLE

150 g (½ cup) tomato paste
4 tbsp extra virgin olive oil
1 tbsp salt-packed capers
2 tbsp anchovy paste
3 tbsp red wine vinegar
a few bay leaves

Combine the oil and tomato paste in a small pot.
Finely chop the capers. As soon as the tomato paste starts to heat, add the capers, the anchovy paste, the red wine vinegar and the bay leaves. Cook on low heat for about 5 minutes.

This sauce keeps well in the fridge for several days. It is also very good as a dipping sauce for crudités.

TORTA DI RISO, PATATE E PECORINO

Rice, Potato and Pecorino Cheese Tart

from Castelnuovo di Garfagnana's Market

At Osteria Il Vecchio Mulino they serve a similar savory tart with their cured meats and cheese platter. This version is not unlike the savory rice tart of Lunigiana and nearby Liguria. Make this for an evening meal on your backyard patio among friends. Serve slightly warm, accompanied by hearty salads, soft cheeses and cured meats.

INGREDIENTS FOR 4 PEOPLE

FOR THE FILLING
50 g (¾ cup) originario rice
300 g (⅔ lb) potatoes
250 g (1 cup) cow's milk ricotta
60 g (⅔ cup) grated pecorino cheese
1 egg
salt
pepper

FOR THE DOUGH
400 g (3 & ¼ cups) all-purpose flour
100 g (¾ cup) whole wheat flour
½ cup oil
½ cup white wine
1 egg yolk for the glaze
salt

Start by making the filling. Peel and cube the potatoes. Boil the potatoes together with the rice in plenty of salted water. Drain the rice and potatoes and combine with the ricotta and grated pecorino. Beat the egg and add it to the mixture. Adjust for salt and pepper.

Next prepare the dough. Pour the two flours onto a pastry board. Add the salt. Gradually pour in the oil and the wine, using a fork to mix at the start.

Knead until a smooth and elastic dough forms. Divide the dough into two portions, with one slightly larger than the other.

Roll out the larger portion of dough with a rolling pin, using a small amount of flour as needed. Grease a baking dish 26 cm in diameter (about 10 inches) and lay in the rolled out dough. Puncture the bottom of the dough with a fork, then add the filling.

Roll out the second portion of dough and carefully place it on top of the tart. Seal the edges well and cut away the excess dough. Puncture the top of the tart with a fork. Glaze with the beaten egg yolk.

Bake at 180°C/350°F for around 50 to 55 minutes, until golden. Serve hot or tepid, alongside cured meats and cheeses.

NECCI CON UOVA E RIGATINO

Chestnut Crêpes with Egg and Rigatino Pancetta

from Piazza della Sala Market in Pistoia

Castagnaccio is a specialty cake much in keeping with the reserved, uncomplicated nature of Tuscan cuisine, made with only chestnut flour, water, olive oil, rosemary, raisins and pine nuts. Nothing could seem simpler—that is, until you try *necci* for the first time. I myself did not know what they were until a few years ago, since typical snacks for me had always been grilled bread topped with olive oil in winter, bread with tomato in summer and, often enough, tea with cookies. These were the flavors of my afternoons, flavors that conjure up memories of a full belly and a happy childhood, of a grandmother and mother who raised me on simple, good things. Chestnut flour, however, the base ingredient of *necci*, was not an item regularly found in our pantry. These thin crêpes originate in the Garfagnana area and the Pistoia Mountains. They are served either immediately on their own, or filled with sausage, pancetta or sheep milk ricotta. Their fascinating preparation method requires a lively fire and two flat cast iron pans called *testi*, between which the *necci* batter is spread. The pans are then placed on the fire to heat up both sides. Traditionally the *testi* pans would have been greased with a small amount of lard, but today a quality olive oil is used instead. Once cooked, *necci* were stacked up, separated by chestnut leaves, ready to be eaten according to one's preference. While characteristic of the *cucina povera*, *necci* are also intriguingly modern, being both gluten- and sugar-free. Their quick preparation requires no resting time. Lacking a set of *testi*, the only requirement is a good non-stick pan. The sweet chestnut flour pairs well with the savory *rigatino* and sausage, while the egg yolk brings all the flavors together.

INGREDIENTS FOR 4 PEOPLE

400 g (3 & 1/3 cups) chestnut flour
450 ml (1 & 3/4 cups) water
1 pinch of salt
extra virgin olive oil for the pan
4 eggs
2 sausages
8 slices *rigatino* (pancetta)

Pour the chestnut flour into a mixing bowl and add a pinch of salt. Slowly pour in the water, mixing continuously with a whisk to prevent lumps, until a smooth batter forms. Grease a non-stick pan with a drizzle of olive oil and heat on medium. When the pan is hot, pour a ladleful of batter onto the center of the pan.

Tilt the pan to evenly distribute the batter. Let the crêpe cook until it starts to bubble and come away from the pan. Flip the crêpe with a spatula and brown on the other side. Arrange the *necci* on a plate as you proceed.

Break up the sausage and brown it in a non-stick pan. Break an egg on top and cook it until the whites are firm and the yolk soft.

Brown the sliced *rigatino* and serve with the egg, sausage and *necci*.

PREMIATA DITTA BARTOLETTI
CAFFE' GIUSTI
CASA FONDATA NEL 1898
CAFFETTERIA
GELATI
CIOCCOLATA CALDA
FRAGOLE CON PANNA
LIQUORI
VINI
BIRRA PUNCH
COCTAILS
PRIMI PIATTI
SECONDI PIATTI
Polenta con funghi
Trippa alla fiorentina
CUCINA
TRADIZIONA
VINI

LA FETTUNTA

Grilled Bread with Olive Oil

We were seated in the hall of the Hotel Maria in Montecatini Terme, at a round table covered with cool drinks to temper a sudden and unexpected early-May heatwave. We talked like old friends in that room that felt like something out of the past. And yet we had just met Maria, her family and her friends, a few minutes before. Some days prior, an American woman named Paulina had contacted me through my blog, asking for information on some traditional recipes from my region. After an epistolary exchange worthy of a former era, I discovered that Paulina had a cousin named Maria, who owned a delightful hotel in Montecatini Terme.

Perhaps fate wanted Montecatini to be the next stop on our exploration of Tuscan markets. And thus we found ourselves seated together, our glasses of ice tea in hand, talking about historic recipes and local ingredients in between bouts of laughter. With a few quick phone calls, Maria had managed to bring together local food experts and friends with similar gourmet interests, and I felt I had been unexpectedly drawn into a high-society salon from the turn of the last century.
We talked of everything, from the best kind of Montecatini wafer cookies to *pollo in camicia nera* (recipe on page 264) and savory croissants. Interestingly, although most known for its thermal spas, Montecatini was also the birthplace of the *cornetto salato*, or salted croissant, created by the Pellegrini family in the 1920s and '30s.

But the thing that piqued my curiosity most was a description of an unusual *aperitivo* (a pre-meal drink sometimes accompanied by light finger foods). From Montecatini Terme head up towards Montecatini *vecchia* (the old part of town) to take the late 19th-century funicular—two small, vintage-style red trains that connect Castello to the spas, each equipped with three compartments featuring wooden benches and small outer balconies. The views are breathtaking.

After your ascent, wander through the medieval streets and alleyways to arrive at Caffè Giusti for a drink, where you simply must try the *fettunta col prosciutto crudo* (recipe follows), or olive oil bruschetta with prosciutto.

FETTUNTA COL PROSCIUTTO CRUDO

Olive Oil Bruschetta with Prosciutto

from Montecatini Earth Market

Two of my favorite childhood snacks are mixed in the *fettunta col prosciutto crudo* served at Caffè Giusti in Montecatini *vecchia*: *pane e olio*, toasted bread doused with good extra virgin olive oil, and *pane e prosciutto*, a slice of bread topped with some prosciutto.
Together they take bruschetta to a higher level, and justify the disproportionate size of the bread slabs served at Caffè Giusti. It is never enough.

INGREDIENTS FOR 4 PEOPLE

4 slices of Tuscan bread
1 garlic clove
extra virgin olive oil
salt
100 g Tuscan prosciutto crudo

Toast the bread until charred in spots.

Rub it with a clove of garlic, drizzle it generously with olive oil and salt it sparingly, then drape the prosciutto crudo on top.

Do not linger any longer and enjoy it immediately.

SPUMA DI MORTADELLA

Mortadella Pâté

from Prato's Market

The spicy, old-world aroma of Prato mortadella stands out at this market. Visit Mannori's cured meats stand for a veritable explosion of salamis, hand-sliced prosciutto, flat or rolled pancetta porchetta and, above all, *la mortadella di Prato.*

This is an economic type of cured meat, boiled and encased, and made from parts discarded in the processing of *finocchiona* and salami. Ingredients like ground garlic, pepper, coriander, cinnamon and cloves account for its intense spiced flavor.

The slightly red color of this mortadella comes from Alchermes, a liqueur produced by Florence's Farmacia di Santa Maria Novella. The use of Alchermes in this recipe represents an interesting double historical link between Florence and Prato, as the dye obtained from the cochineal, or Kermes, insect is what gives the Florentine liqueur drink—and thus the Prato mortadella—its red color, but moreover it also was formerly used to dye fabrics.

The butchers of Prato, or *beccai,* have been making mortadella since at least the 18th century: the first documentation of this cured meat dates to 1733, when it was served as a local specialty at the beatification feast of Sister Caterina de' Ricci.

After World War II, Prato mortadella nearly vanished, leaving in its place other more sought-after meats. In recent years, however, thanks to the combined efforts of local salami producers, mortadella has returned to reclaim its historic and traditional birthplace. Today it is a Slow Food Presidium, and in 2016 it earned IGP status. Prato mortadella is traditionally served with Carmignano figs (from the nearby town of the same name) along with the local bread, *la bozza pratese.* Its characteristically Renaissance spiciness goes well with risottos, or with this mortadella pâté, inspired by the Bolognese version. Serve as a spread for crostini, small slices of toasted bread.

INGREDIENTS FOR 8 PEOPLE

- 300 g (10 & ½ oz) Prato mortadella (or Bologna mortadella)
- 300 g (10 & ½ oz) fresh sheep milk ricotta
- 50 ml (¼ cup) whipping cream
- 1 tbsp grated Parmigiano cheese

Finely chop the mortadella and transfer to a mixer or blender along with the ricotta, cream and Parmigiano cheese.

Blend the ingredients until you have a smooth and creamy mousse.

COCCOLI

Fried Dough Balls

from Marradi's Market

Florentines are often heard saying, "Shall we go and have a few *coccoli*?" Especially in winter, when fried, warm and crunchy treats are irresistible. When these little clouds of dough are then accompanied by a soft cheese and aged prosciutto, they become the perfect way to start off a Tuscan meal among friends.
The first time I heard people talking about *coccoli* in Florence I exclaimed, "Oh, you mean fried *topi*!"—*topi*, meaning "mice", is another nickname for fried dough balls, at least outside of Florence. My friends looked at me with a mix of horror and dismay.
At my house fried dough balls were always known as *zonzelle*, similar to *coccoli* except for the shape: elongated rather than round. Just out of the frying oil, they are heavily salted and eaten as a snack at birthday parties or as a starter dish when you have some leftover dough to use up.
In Florence and Mugello, *coccoli* are made with a dough similar to the one used to make the *topi* of my childhood, which are likewise paired with prosciutto and stracchino cheese. I will admit, though, that my favorite way to eat them is covered in *burrata*, a concession to my Tuscan roots.
You'll find *coccoli* in most trattorias but more likely at a *sagra*, where, seated with friends in that fun and laid back setting one consumes infinite amounts of homemade specialties: starting with *coccoli*, then on to a brimming plate of *tortelli* with meat sauce, then roasted meats. Lastly comes the requisite glass of *amaro*, or bitter liqueur, to help the digestive system do its job.

INGREDIENTS FOR 4 PEOPLE

500 g (4 cups) all-purpose flour
350 ml (1 & ½ cups) water
10 g (1 & ⅔ tsp) salt
15 g (1 tbsp) extra virgin olive oil
2 g (⅛ oz) fresh yeast
peanut oil for frying

TO ACCOMPANY THE COCCOLI
prosciutto crudo
stracchino cheese

Dissolve the yeast in ⅔ of the water. Transfer to a stand mixer bowl and add the flour. Knead for about 5 minutes until the dough is elastic. Add the salt and continue to knead for another 10 minutes while gradually adding the remaining water.

Lastly add the oil and knead for another 5 minutes.

Place the dough in a bowl greased with oil, cover with plastic wrap and let ripen on the refrigerator's least cold shelf for about 24 hours.

Remove the dough from the fridge and let it go to room temperature.

Form balls with the dough that are more or less the size of an apricot. Fry in batches in plenty of hot oil, turning them frequently.

Remove from the oil when puffed and golden. Drain well and salt. Serve with the prosciutto and stracchino.

IL LARDO DI GOMBITELLI

Gombitelli Lardo

The hamlet of Gombitelli in the Camaiore municipality is considered a linguistic island. According to some, the Gallo-Romance language spoken for centuries in this small town arrived in the Middle Ages with artisan knife sharpeners immigrating from Piedmont, while for others it was blacksmiths from Bergamo who introduced the language. Other theories place the arrival of the Gallo-Romance language in more recent periods, attributing it to a group of German *Landsknechts* (mercenary soldiers) who arrived in the 16th century and settled into professions such as blacksmithing and knife manufacturing and sharpening. The most likely explanation, however, is found in the arrival of iron-working families from the Tosco-Emiliano Apennines, who led an isolated life in Gombitelli and were known to keep to themselves.

More to the point here, however, is the profession these "invaders" all likely shared: namely, iron working and knife manufacturing, professions that would have made them master cutters. It's easy to imagine then how their skills would easily transfer to those relied on by *norcini*, or pork butchers.

Today the village of Gombitelli is home to just over 100 souls, and yet it boasts three *norcini* butchers who work their raw materials following traditional methods.
The artisan salami producers at the Salumificio Artigianale Gombitelli shop are located just at the town's entrance.

Run by the Triglia family, the business has been producing salami and other cured meats for centuries, according to ancient family recipes passed down through generations and following traditional craft techniques.
The lardo they produce is sweet and delicate. Just sliced, its shades of pink are the first thing you notice, the characteristic that gives this product both its name and its tenderness. A slice of Gombitelli lardo literally melts in your mouth.

The strips of pork fatback with the lean parts still intact are cured in enormous vats with a mix of salt and spices, including garlic, rosemary, pepper, nutmeg and clove. After the first 20 days of salt-curing, the "mother" brine from previous curing is added (similar to vinegar making and sourdough). The lardo is then left to age for at least 10 months more, until it becomes as soft as butter and intensely flavored.

LARDO ROSA MARINATO

Marinated Pink Lard

from Camaiore's Market

L*ardo*, a typical charcuterie product from Tuscany, is the fat of the back of the pig, traditionally cured for months in marble basins with salt, pepper, and a mixture of herbs and aromatics.
If you cannot put your hands on the exquisite *lardo rosa*, pink lard, from Gombitelli (see previous page), you can substitute it with an equally excellent lardo di Colonnata.
For a more autumnal version, sauté some radicchio with olive oil with a few pine nuts, let it cool down, lay it on toasted bread, then drape the marinated lardo slices on top.

INGREDIENTS FOR 4 PEOPLE

12 slices of finely cut pink lardo from Gombitelli
1 rosemary sprig
1 garlic clove
chili pepper
extra virgin olive oil
4 slices of Tuscan bread

Arrange the thinly sliced lardo on a tray.

Finely chop the rosemary with the garlic, then scatter the mince on top of the lardo. Add a pinch of chili pepper if you like it. Drizzle with olive oil and let it marinate at room temperature for about a half hour.

In the meantime, toast the bread and let it cool: contrary to the recipes one usually comes across, in this case the lardo should be served cold, without being heated or melted. It is so soft and creamy, in fact, that to be fully enjoyed it must be eaten at room temperature, when it can really give its best. Place the lardo on bread and serve it as an appetizer.

Should you be using lardo di Colonnata instead, serve it on hot bread.

MELITO DI ROSA DELLA SIGNORA GIGLIOLA

Signora Gigliola's Rose Honey

from Santo Spirito's Market in Florence

Giovanni and Gigliola live in Casole d'Elsa and have been family friends for many years now. They make raw honey, apple cider vinegar, mead, royal jelly, propolis and herbal tinctures. Gigliola is our go-to when seasonal bugs hit or we're not feeling well: she always knows how to help us, and welcomes us with her wide, infectious smile, fire-red hair and eyes blue as the sky.
She and Giovanni are regulars at some of Tuscany's organic farmers markets. Their ideas will fascinate you, so if you'd like to meet them, or if you are simply in search of a very nice Tuscan honey, you can find them at the Fierucola market in Piazza Santissima Annunziata or in Santo Spirito, both in Florence.
A few years ago, at a birthday party for one of Gigliola's four children, Elena, I tasted a rose petal honey with an intense floral aroma. It was a kind of honey syrup, which Gigliola makes each year when the roses are at their peak bloom.
It calls for only two ingredients: petals from a heritage red rose, among the most fragrant of roses, and raw honey. It can be paired with soft or aged cheeses, fruit salads, yogurt or ice cream.

INGREDIENTS FOR 500 G JAR

500 g (1 & ½ cups) raw clover honey (or another honey with delicate flavor)
125 g (5 oz) rose petals from an old garden rose variety

Gather the roses in the morning, when they are fresh and fragrant.

Carefully remove the petals and place them in a bowl. Rinse them in cold water and gently dry them. You can use a salad spinner to dry the petals faster.

Chop the petals into small pieces and place them in a pot with the honey. Transfer the pot to a bain marie and melt the honey with the roses. Remove the sauce pan from the water and transfer to low heat.

Bring to a boil and remove from the heat. Let the syrup rest for an hour, then filter.

Pour the filtered syrup into a jar and store in the cupboard or pantry until opened.

CROSTONI CON SPUMA DI GOTA E STRACCHINO

Grilled Bread, Pork Cheek Pâté and Stracchino

from the White Truffle Market Fair in San Miniato

Of all the products available at the Falaschi butcher shop, this pâté made from the cured cheeks of half-wild pigs is my favorite. The meat is ground with a mortar into a creamy soft pâté with a strong, woodsy aroma. Spread it on toasted bread, or add a bit to the pan as you cook chicken breasts or shrimp. Or make these *crostoni*, large slices of grilled bread. The idea here is a twist on the Tuscan classic of grilled bread with sausage and stracchino cheese. It's always a popular starter during my wintertime cooking classes, and there's never enough to satisfy neither young nor old. Stracchino isn't my favorite of cheeses—I prefer types like soft pecorino—but when paired with this pâté the flavors harmonize perfectly.
Serve this as a starter if you prefer, but keep in mind that if you put out a lot, and especially if the *crostoni* are large, no one will have room left for the main course!

INGREDIENTS FOR 4 PEOPLE

200 g (7 oz) pork cheek pâté
250 g (9 oz) stracchino cheese
2 tbsp fennel seeds
8 slices Tuscan bread
freshly ground black pepper

Heat the grill setting to 190°C/375°F.

Combine the pâté, stracchino and fennel seeds in a bowl. Using a fork, smash the mixture to roughly combine all the ingredients.

Slice the bread into thick slices and spread generous amounts of the mixture on each slice. Transfer to the oven and cook under the grill until the cheese is melted and the bread slices are golden at the edges.

Serve immediately while still hot, with a dusting of freshly ground black pepper.

TORTA DI CECI CON LE CIPOLLE

Chickpea Flour Cake with Spring Onions

from the Central Food Market in Livorno

Livornese people would call this not just a *torta,* cake but *the torta,* as for them it's unequaled. And don't call it *cecina,* a dish that, though equal in shape, ingredients, cooking and flavor, comes from Pisa. If you prefer, go ahead and call it *cinque e cinque,* meaning "five and five." In the past, it was customary in Livorno's popular street food scene to order five cents' worth of this *torta* and five cents' worth of bread, usually the long, thin loaf called *francesino* or round, soft *schiacciatina.*

Though best when baked in a wood-fired oven and using large, round copper baking sheets, it can be made at home. Without the heat generated by a wood oven, it won't obtain its characteristic golden crunchiness, but with a very hot oven and heated baking sheet, you can achieve something very close to the original. The traditional way of serving this cake is with a generous dusting of black pepper, inside a sandwich along with a few slices of grilled eggplant. Invariably it will be accompanied by an old favorite, the aromatic soft drink known as *spuma bionda.* So serve it with a glass of *spuma bionda* or something similar, and enjoy. I like to add thinly sliced fresh spring onions to the chickpea cake batter to give it even more flavor.

INGREDIENTS FOR 4 PEOPLE

100 g (1 & ⅛ cups) chickpea flour
300 ml (1 & ¼ cups) water
3 g (½ tsp) salt
2 tbsp extra virgin olive oil
1 spring onions, white part only, thinly sliced
quality seed oil for greasing the baking dish
freshly ground black pepper

Slowly pour the water into the chickpea flour while whisking continuously to prevent lumps. When the water is completely incorporated, add the extra virgin olive oil and salt. Let the batter rest at room temperature for a few hours, after which scoop off the foam that forms on the surface.

Place a round baking sheet about 25 cm (10 inches) in diameter in the oven and set the temperature to maximum. The baking sheet should be very hot when you put the cake in the oven.

Once the sheet is hot, grease it with the oil, pour in the batter to form a thin layer, no more than 3 or 4 mm (about 0.15 inches), and sprinkle with the thinly sliced spring onions. Cook for 20 to 25 minutes at 250°C/475°F, until crunchy and golden on the surface but still soft inside.

Serve the chickpea cake with plenty of freshly ground black pepper.

SOUPS

CARABACCIA

Florentine Onion Soup

from Sant'Ambrogio Market in Florence

When I find myself in front of crates of onions at the market, I often feel an uncontrollable urge: I'm tempted to buy all of them, even if I've already got plenty at home, and despite the hundreds of onions my mother plants in her garden every year, which she then braids and hangs to dry in the garden shed. Onions may indeed make one cry, yet they also provide moments of indescribable joy, as they do when cooked slowly in oil on low heat, releasing an unexpected sweetness that enhances any dish. Onion soup is proof of this.

INGREDIENTS FOR 4 PEOPLE

120 g (⅔ cup) dried split peas
1 kg (2 & ¼ lb) red onions
1 carrot
1 celery stalk
½ cup extra virgin olive oil
1.5 l (1 & ½ qt) chicken stock
4 slices of stale bread
medium-aged Tuscan pecorino cheese

Soak the peas for a few hours before making the soup.

Thinly slice the onions with a very sharp knife or a mandoline slicer. Make a fine mince out of the carrot and celery and place in a large pot with the onion. Add the oil and cook on low for about an hour, until all the liquid is released from the onions.

Next add the previously soaked dried peas and gradually add the stock. Continue cooking for at least a half hour more. The peas should be soft and the soup rather dense.

Ladle the *carabaccia* into 4 ovenproof soup mugs or bowls, then place a slice of stale Tuscan bread on top of each along with a generous dusting of grated pecorino cheese and a drizzle of olive oil.

Transfer to the oven. Cook using the grill function until the cheese melts, forming a golden, stringy crust.

Serve immediately, accompanied by more bread and cheese, if you like.

PAPPA AL POMODORO

My Grandma's Bread and Tomato Soup

from Colle Val d'Elsa Market

Whenever I think of comfort food, the kind that like a warm and soft embrace always makes me feel better, I think of *pappa al pomodoro*.

In Tuscany there are as many *pappa al pomodoro* recipes as households, but they usually converge under two main categories: the Sienese recipe is usually pale in color, made with stale bread and just a few pieces of fresh tomatoes, sage and basil.

The Florentine-style *pappa al pomodoro* calls instead for *battuto* (finely minced carrots, and tomato purée), resulting in a more vibrant red color, different from my grandmother's version. Cooking class after cooking class, summer after summer, I finally settled on my own pappa al pomodoro recipe, a blend of the Florentine and the Sienese recipes—just like me, and just like Val d'Elsa.

INGREDIENTS FOR 4 PEOPLE

4 ripe Roma tomatoes
120 ml (½ cup) extra virgin olive oil
4 garlic cloves
dried chili pepper
4 thick slices of stale Tuscan bread, torn into large pieces
a handful of basil leaves
salt

Pappa al pomodoro will turn out much smoother if you peel the tomatoes (and you won't be left with bits of tomato skin in your teeth). Plunge the tomatoes into a large pot of boiling water for 30 seconds. Remove them quickly and transfer to a bowl of cold water. The skin will come away easily. Peel and deseed the tomatoes, then chop them in half. Set aside.

Pour the oil into a large pot, add the crushed garlic cloves, and sautée on medium heat until fragrant. Add the torn bread and cook for about 5 minutes until golden.

Now add the reserved chopped tomatoes and a handful of fresh basil leaves, then cook on medium heat for about 5 minutes. When the bread softens up a bit, cover with water and cook on medium heat for about 10 minutes, stirring vigorously from time to time with a whisk to obtain its characteristic creamy, smooth texture. Taste and adjust the seasoning with salt.

Let the *pappa al pomodoro* rest for at least an hour, after which you can reheat it on low if you wish to serve it warm. Otherwise serve at room temperature.

PASSATO DI ZUCCA E CECI

Butternut Squash and Chickpea Purée

from the Farmers Market in Siena

The first organic farmers market came to my home town Colle Val d'Elsa about fifteen years ago. Upon reading the news, I could barely contain myself! A local farmers market, the chances it offered—to buy directly from area producers and speak with them, to touch the variety of seasonal products with my own hands—was a dream come true. It was at this very market I started my first cooking classes for children, held inside a large tent in the town square.

We would meet one Sunday a month. First we would do the shopping, browsing the stands and filling up wicker baskets at times larger than the children themselves. Then we would cook together, our goal being to introduce children to seasonal fruit and vegetables and demonstrate how something formerly unknown to them could be transformed into something tasty.

INGREDIENTS FOR 4 PEOPLE

FOR THE PURÉE

600 g (1 & ⅓ lb) butternut squash
1 leek, finely sliced
3 tbsp extra virgin olive oil
600 g (1 & ⅓ lb) chickpeas, cooked
600 ml (2 & ½ cups) chickpea cooking liquid
fine sea salt
black pepper
nutmeg

TO SERVE

2 tbsp extra virgin olive oil
4 tbsp mixed seeds
a handful sage leaves
4 tbsp full-fat yogurt

Peel the squash, cube the flesh and place in a large casserole pot along with the oil and leek. Cook on medium heat for about 25 minutes, stirring frequently to flavor the squash and prevent the leek from burning (which would result in a bitter flavor).

Next add the chickpeas and their cooking liquids. Cook for another 15 minutes, stirring occasionally. Process the entire mixture. Adjust for salt and pepper and add a pinch of grated nutmeg.

In a small pan toast the seeds with oil and sage leaves until shiny.

Serve the soup with a dollop of yogurt, a drizzle of olive oil, and the toasted seeds.

PASTA E FAGIOLI

Pasta and Beans

Florentines are often called by the nickname *mangiafagioli*, meaning "bean eaters", given their immense love for these legumes. In truth, however, all Tuscans are fond of beans, and each obviously has his or her favorite: the red beans of Lucca known as *lo scritto*, cannellini or zolfini. And farmers markets are just the place to find beans characteristic of the area. Often they are packaged in plastic bags that include a few recipe ideas.

Given their protein content, beans are a worthwhile substitute for meat, and as such feature in numerous so-called "peasant" recipes, from *fagioli all'uccelletto* to bean purée with sage, olive oil and a hint of tomato for color. Beans can be cooked in a *fiasco*—a repurposed large glass wine bottle—or in terracotta pots left to cook overnight in the embers of a wood-fired oven.

Beans also announce the arrival of "new" or fresh-pressed olive oil, which will be generously drizzled over grilled bread topped with juicy cooked kale. We are so fond of these legumes that we decided to dedicate the cover of this book to this recipe (see on page 196)

Pasta and beans is actually a traditional southern dish, yet at my house it is a classic winter's day dish, along with pasta and potatoes and pasta and chickpeas.

PASTA DI FARRO E FAGIOLI ZOLFINI

Spelt Pasta and Zolfini Beans

from the First Earth Market in Montevarchi

This recipe calls for zolfini beans, a flavorful variety from the Pratomagno area with a very fine skin and thick, creamy texture. Their name owes to their pale yellow color, similar to sulphur, or *zolfo* in Italian. Zolfini beans are cooked on low heat for two or three hours, without pre-soaking.
On their own they make a delicious meal, even more so when garnished with a drizzle of good olive oil, salt and freshly ground black pepper.

INGREDIENTS FOR 4 PEOPLE

½ carrot
½ celery stalk
½ white onion
3 tbsp extra virgin olive oil
50 g (1 & ¾ oz) pancetta
600 g (3 & ⅓ cups) cooked zolfini beans
600 ml (2 & ½ cups) of the beans' cooking liquid
1 tbsp tomato paste
160 g (5 & ½ oz) short spelt pasta
salt
freshly ground black pepper

Make a mince by finely chopping the carrot, celery and onion. Finely chop the pancetta. Sautée all in olive oil for 5 minutes on low heat in a heavy bottom pot.

Add the beans and their cooking liquid together with a tablespoon of tomato paste. Adjust for salt.

Bring to a boil and cook on medium heat. Add the pasta and cook according to the package instructions, stirring periodically.

As soon as the pasta is cooked, remove the pot from the heat.
The beans will bring creaminess to this dish, so there's no need to add cheese. Serve with a drizzle of olive oil and a bit of freshly ground black pepper.

VELLUTATA DI PORRI CON LA TARESE

Leek Purée with "Tarese" Pancetta

from the First Earth Market in Montevarchi

For something really special in Montevarchi, I recommend a short road trip to Menchetti, on the road that leads to San Giovanni Valdarno. The family-run Menchetti business has been making naturally leavened breads for three generations, using heritage Verna wheat, grown and stone ground in Valdichiana.
It was with them I tasted this purée, a soup of leeks and potatoes creamed with a small amount of chicken broth, without butter or cream. Make this in winter. It's like a warm embrace that envelops you in a sense of well-being. The star ingredient is *la tarese*, a pancetta of unusual size that today is a Slow Food presidium, born from the need to use as much of the adult pig as possible in a time when the only way to conserve pork was to cure it with salt. *Tarese* is made from cuts of the pork back and the stomach, from animals that weigh more than 200 kg (440 pounds), and includes a part of the more desirable cut, the loin. It's seasoned with pepper, red garlic, juniper and other Tuscan spices often kept secret by the butchers who prepare it, and preserved in coarse salt. It has a strong flavor and spicy fragrance but above all a uniquely soft texture owing to the loin fats. In the past it would have be grilled and served together with winter radicchio or zolfini beans. Today it's more a refined *hors d'oeuvre*, sliced very thin and layered on top of grilled bread.

INGREDIENTS FOR 4 PEOPLE

4 medium leeks
200 g (½ lb) yellow potatoes
4 tbsp extra virgin olive oil
500 g (2 cups) chicken stock
salt
black pepper
2 thin slices of Valdarno *tarese* (or pancetta)
4 slices toasted bread

WHERE TO BUY VALDARNO TARESE:
Macelleria Mauro Cioni (butcher), located at Piazza Roanne 9, Montevarchi (AR).
Macelleria Marco Fantechi (butcher), located in Via Burzagli 116, Montevarchi (AR).
Antica Macelleria Norcineria Fabbrini (butcher), Via Roma 7, San Giovanni Valdarno (AR).

Rinse the leeks to remove any residual dirt. Slice into thin rounds, using both the white and tender green parts. Peel the potatoes and cut into uniform cubes.

Pour a few tablespoons of olive oil into a casserole dish. Add the potatoes and leeks and cook on medium heat, stirring from time to time, for 5 minutes.

Pour in the chicken stock and cook for about 20 minutes on low heat, until the potatoes are very soft and a fork punctures them very easily.

Process with a food mill or immersion blender and return to the heat. Adjust for salt and pepper.

Slice the *tarese* or pancetta into thin strips and brown it in a pan for a few minutes until they turn crunchy.

Toast the bread and serve the purée in four soup bowls topped with the crunchy strips of cured meat, a drizzle of olive oil and freshly ground black pepper.

ZUPPA DI FARRO DELLA GARFAGNANA

Garfagnana Farro Soup

from Castelnuovo di Garfagnana's Market

Farro is one of the oldest grains cultivated by man, known since the 7th century B.C. in Mesopotamia, Syria, Egypt and Palestine. It later became a staple food among Latin populations, who used the flour to make polenta and focaccia breads. This protein- and vitamin-rich grain is a slow release energy food. For this reason it was prized among the Roman military. It was farro, in fact, not iron, that facilitated the Roman conquest of the world and the creation of an empire! With the introduction of other grain varieties, however, farro cultivation gradually disappeared, with the exception of some few areas that have carried on the tradition.
Farro has been cultivated in Tuscany since time immemorial, and continuously so in Garfagnana, where nearly 100 farms produce the Garfagnana IGP variety—a unique product that reflects the significant relationship of land, climate and altitude. It's the base ingredient of many recipes from the *cucina povera* tradition (meaning "poor" or peasant cooking), such as farro soup, farro with beans and sweet farro tart.
The farro soup of Garfagnana seems to have come straight out of the pages of history. This unique, flavorful and well-balanced dish typically calls for a local variety of bean, such lo scritto (red and white), but you can use cannellini or borlotti beans instead.

INGREDIENTS FOR 6 PEOPLE

250 g (½ lb) red beans from Lucca (or other)
½ red onion
2 tbsp extra virgin olive oil
50 g (1 & ¾ oz) pancetta
350 g (10 & ½ oz) farro
500 g (just over 1 lb) potatoes
a few sage leaves
salt
pepper

Soak the beans overnight in a bowl of water.

Drain the beans the next day. Finely chop the onion with the pancetta. Transfer the mince to a large, heavy bottom pot with a few tablespoons of olive oil and cook on low for a few minutes.

When the onion has softened, add the drained beans. Combine well and pour in at least 2 l of water (just over 4 pints). Add a pinch of salt but not too much. You will adjust for salt later.

Simmer uncovered on low heat for about an hour. Peel and roughly cube the potatoes and add to the pot along with the farro and a few sage leaves. Cook on low for another hour, until the soup becomes thick and creamy. Add small amounts of hot water as needed, should the soup become dry. Now adjust for salt, if needed, and serve with a drizzle of olive oil and freshly ground black pepper.

POLENTA CON LE LEGHE

Polenta with Tuscan Kale

from Piazza della Sala Market in Pistoia

This polenta is often cooked directly in the cooking liquids of red or *borlotti* beans. Another fundamental ingredient is kale, arguably the most popular leafy green during the Tuscan winter. And, in fact, the best time to make this recipe is winter, after the first frost, when kale leaves are at their most tender and crunchy. The *leghe* here, meaning "bonds" or "ties", are the strips of kale that "hold" the polenta together. It can be eaten in two ways: served immediately while still warm, or sliced and reheated in a pan the following day.
The beans are a local variety from Lucca that break apart easily when cooked, making them ideal for soups, yet any type of red bean can be used. The corn flour used here is called *bramata*, indicating a large grain flour (as opposed to *fioretto*, or *fine*), as this dish requires time. A small amount of tomato is called for to cook the kale.

INGREDIENTS FOR 4 PEOPLE

500 g (just over 1 lb) red beans from Lucca (or other red bean)
1 bunch kale
extra virgin olive oil
1 garlic clove
½ red onion
2 ripe tomatoes, peeled
300 g (2 cups) coarse grain corn flour
salt

Soak the beans overnight in plenty of water. Drain and transfer to a large pot with a quantity of water 3 to 4 times their volume. Bring to the boil and cook for about 2 hours, until the beans are soft.

Thoroughly rinse the kale leaves. Cut away their stems and slice the leaves into thin strips. Add a tablespoon of olive oil to a pot. Chop the garlic and onion and cook for a few minutes. Roughly chop the peeled tomato and add to the pot along with the strips of kale.

Cook for about 30 minutes on low heat, stirring occasionally.

Process half the beans with 2 cups of their cooking liquid until smooth. Add the creamed beans to the kale.

Gradually pour in the corn flour, stirring continuously to prevent any lumps.

Add a liter of the remaining cooking liquid to the pot a little at a time. Cook on low for about 40 minutes, stirring occasionally. Adjust for salt towards the end of the cooking time. Add the remaining beans without their liquid and combine to obtain a creamy polenta. Serve immediately garnished with a drizzle of olive oil.

GARMUGÌA

Vegetable and Legume Soup

from the Farmers Market at the Ancient Forum Boarium in Lucca

You hear a lot of talk about micro-seasonality, of ingredients that appear—or seem to appear—at market stands for a mere few days before disappearing and making one wait another year to see them again. Some examples include *agretti*, broad beans and fresh peas...
Garmugìa is one of those recipes that can only be made during a specific time of year, when broad beans, peas, asparagus and artichokes are all in season. It's a soup bursting with the colors and flavors of spring.
Make plenty of it, and often, while you can, because soon enough the ingredients will be out of season and you'll have to wait another year to taste it.
Don't be mislead by its appearance. This is no simple vegetable *minestrone*, but rather a hearty, fortifying soup.

INGREDIENTS FOR 4 PEOPLE

2 spring onions
extra virgin olive oil
50 g (1 & ¾ oz) pancetta
150 g (5 oz) ground beef
100 g (3 & ½ oz) peeled broad beans
100 g (3 & ½ oz) shelled fresh peas
100 g (3 & ½ oz) asparagus
4 artichokes
1 l (4 cups) vegetable broth
salt
freshly ground black pepper
4 slices of stale bread

Prep all the vegetables so they are ready when you begin cooking.

Shell the broad beans and the peas. Slice the asparagus into rounds, leaving the tips whole. Clean and thinly slice the artichokes, and soak them in lemon water to keep from turning brown.

Finely slice the whites of the spring onions. Place the onion slices in a large pot with a few tablespoons of oil. Cut the pancetta into strips and add to the pot. Sauté the onion and then add the ground meat. Stir well with a spoon to cook the meat evenly. When the meat begins to sizzle, add all the prepped vegetables. Combine well to season and then pour in the warm broth.

Lightly season with salt and pepper. Cover and cook on medium-low heat for about 30 minutes, until the vegetables are tender but not coming apart.

Meanwhile, cut the stale bread into cubes and toast them in a pan with a few tablespoons of oil. Serve with the toasted bread and a drizzle of olive oil.

ACQUACOTTA

Maremma Style Vegetable Soup

from the Smaller Markets in Capalbio

This is one of the Maremma's most traditional dishes, an ancient, peasant-style soup made from the simple, economical ingredients a farmer's wife would have on hand: water, stale bread, and a few vegetables from the garden or foraged in the countryside.

While touring around Maremma and enjoying a variety of traditional meals—whether seated in the arbor of a *trattoria* or around a local family's table—you will come across countless versions of *acquacotta,* each influenced by seasonality, the traits of a particular area, and the individual flair of the cook. Yet all versions reflect certain ideas about essentials, in both ingredients and cooking method.

These days fresh eggs and pecorino cheese are often used in *acquacotta*. I still remember a version served at a dinner held at an organic agritourism structure near Pitigliano. Made with herbs and bitter greens foraged in the woods, it included just-laid eggs and a generous spoonful of sheep milk ricotta. A dusting of grated pecorino cheese completed the masterpiece.

Compared to the classic Tuscan version, this recipe does not contain carrots because, as the cook Ilena pointed out, it would render the *acquacotta* too sweet. Basil and chili pepper are included in the mince, as with many Maremma recipes.

INGREDIENTS FOR 4 PEOPLE

3 yellow onions
4 celery stalks
5 basil leaves, broken up
dried chili pepper
5 tbsp extra virgin olive oil
1 cup white wine
800 g peeled tomatoes
2 l (just over 2 qt) warm water
salt
4 eggs
4 slices of stale bread
aged Tuscan pecorino cheese

Make a mince of the onion and celery. Brown for about 10 minutes in olive oilon low heat together with the basil leaves and a piece of dried chili pepper (to your taste).

Pour in the white wine and cook off the liquid on low heat for another 10 minutes.

Break up the tomatoes with your hands and add to the mixture along with the water. Stir and adjust for salt. Cook on very low heat for about 1 hour, stirring from time to time to keep it from drying out too much.

When the soup is ready, crack in the eggs. Cover the pot and let the whites of the eggs cook.

Serve the acquacotta by placing a slice of bread in a bowl, covered with an egg cooked in the soup and tomato all around it.

The final touch is a generous dusting of pecorino cheese.

FIRST COURSES

CRESPELLE ALLA FIORENTINA

Florentine Crêpes

from Sant'Ambrogio Market in Florence

In the fall, these crêpes are filled with roasted pumpkin, ricotta and nutmeg, or with a mixture of porcini mushrooms and calamint. In the spring, try a filling of asparagus or peas along with some ricotta and sautéed pancetta. The traditional ricotta and spinach filling seasoned with the ever-important nutmeg—said to be so dear to Caterina de' Medici—simply cannot be outdone. For a rustic touch, use whole wheat flour and plenty of pecorino cheese.

INGREDIENTS FOR 4 PEOPLE

FOR THE CRÊPES
3 eggs
3 level tbsp of whole wheat flour
1 pinch of salt
250 ml (1 cup) whole milk

FOR THE FILLING
400 g (¾ lb) fresh spinach
1 tbsp extra virgin olive oil
1 garlic clove
250 g (1 cup) fresh sheep's milk ricotta
100 g (1 cup) aged Tuscan pecorino cheese, grated
150 g (5 oz) medium-aged Tuscan pecorino cheese, cubed
1 pinch of salt
grated nutmeg
1 egg

FOR THE BÉCHAMEL SAUCE
50 g (3 & ½ tbsp) butter
60 g (½ cup) whole wheat flour
500 ml (2 cups) milk
1 pinch of salt
grated nutmeg

TO GARNISH
grated pecorino
tomato sauce
extra virgin olive oil

Make the crêpes batter at least a hour prior. Beat the eggs together with the salt and whole wheat flour, being sure to dissolve all the lumps. Slowly pour in the milk and blend well.

For the filling, blanch the spinach for 5 minutes, drain and squeeze well to remove excess liquid. Finely chop the cooked spinach and sauté them for a few minutes in a tablespoon of oil and the garlic clove. Transfer to a bowl and add the ricotta, the grated and cubed pecorino, the nutmeg and salt. Combine and taste. Add the beaten egg.

Make the béchamel by first melting the butter in a saucepan. When the butter has melted, add the flour and combine with a whisk for a few minutes until it starts to just turn brown in color and loses its raw aroma.

Slowly pour in the cold milk while mixing continuously to prevent lumps. Let the sauce cook for a few minutes until it thickens, then adjust for salt and nutmeg. Heat a greased crêpe pan (14–15 cm or 6 inches in diameter) and cook the crêpes on medium heat for a few minutes on each side, or until golden.

Spread some of the creamed spinach and ricotta mixture on each and roll into a tube shape, as if making cannelloni. Lightly cover the bottom of a casserole dish with some of the béchamel then arrange the crêpes in the dish.

Cover the crêpes with the remaining béchamel, a few tablespoons of tomato sauce, more grated pecorino and a drizzle of olive oil.

Bake at 200°C/400°F for around 20 minutes, or until the crêpes turn golden on the surface and the béchamel and cheese start to bubble on the sides. Serve warm, just out of the oven. Any leftovers can be warmed up (add a small amount of milk).

PICI CON SALSICCIA E CHIANTI

Pici Pasta with Sausage and Chianti Wine

from Pienza's Market

I've been making homemade pici for years, but after I came to know Luisa's version, my own way of preparing them changed drastically. This is the perfectly efficient and practical method she taught me.

INGREDIENTS FOR 4 PEOPLE

FOR THE PICI
250 g (1 cup) water
1 tbsp extra virgin olive oil
1 pinch of salt
500 g (4 cups) all-purpose flour
semolina flour and corn flour
for flouring the pici

FOR THE SAUCE
2 red onions
2 tbsp extra virgin olive oil
4 Tuscan sausages
(about 400 g/14 oz total)
1 glass Chianti wine
grated pecorino cheese

NOTE: Pici should be cooked as soon as they are made. They tend to stick to each other so use plenty of flour to assist. Pici can be freezed as soon as they are made. Remove them from the freezer and transfer directly to boiling water.

Pour the water into a large bowl with the oil and salt. Start to add in the flour while mixing with a fork. When the dough becomes too hard to stir, dump onto a wooden pastry board and proceed kneading by hand, until all the flour is incorporated. Work the ingredients forcefully until you have a smooth, opaque white and firm dough. Cover the dough with the bowl and let rest on the work surface for at least a half hour.

Meanwhile, prepare the sauce. Finely slice the onions and cook them in 2 tbsp oil on low heat for 10 to 15 minutes, until they start to break apart. Keep the heat low to prevent burning.

Remove the casings from the sausages, crumble the meat with your hands and cook with the onions for about 10 minutes. Break up the pieces of sausage into smaller pieces using a wooden spoon.

Add the red wine and cook on low until the wine reduces. This will take about 15 minutes.

Now make the pici. On a clean pastry board, roll out the pasta dough to ½ cm thickness (just under ¼ inch). Moisten the dough with oil to keep it from drying out while you make the pici.

Using a pizza cutter, cut the dough into strips about ½ cm in width. With one hand hold each strip down on one side, and using the other hand roll the strip into a pici shape.

Keep a bowl nearby with a mix of corn flour and durum wheat semolina and dip the ends of the pici into the mix as you proceed.

Once each pici is made, roll it up and place on a tray. Proceed until you have finished the dough.

Cook the pici in plenty of salted boiling water for 5 to 6 minutes and serve with the sauce and a dusting of grated pecorino.

TAGLIATELLE DI CASTAGNE CON SUGO DI NOCI

Chestnut Flour Tagliatelle with Walnut Sauce

from Fivizzano's Market

Fresh pasta is like a touchstone. It centers you in a precise moment, place, and tradition, at a table of guests speaking a specific dialect or accent. In the Mugello region, a border land characterized by scarcity, the simplest pasta filling calls for boiled potato and garlic. In the Maremma, the local version of ravioli are made with borage, evidence of a sustenance economy that relies on foraging.

In the Lunigiana, pasta is sometimes termed *bastarda,* meaning "illegitimate" in that the wheat flour is cut with a portion of chestnut flour.

Knead the dough by hand until it is smooth and silky. This fresh pasta can be cooked as soon as it's rolled out, or left to dry near a stove or other source of heat. When completely dried, the pasta can be stored in paper bags for months, ready to be cooked and seasoned. The following fresh pasta and sauce recipe comes courtesy of Mariangela of the Antico Mulino Rossi mill, who described the method and ingredients to me while we maneuvered between the stone mill and sacks of chestnut flour.

INGREDIENTS FOR 6 PEOPLE

FOR THE TAGLIATELLE

375 g (3 cups) all-purpose flour
125 g (1 cup) chestnut flour
semolina to dust the pasta sheets
1 tbsp extra virgin olive oil
1 pinch of salt
about 250 ml (1 cup) water

FOR THE SAUCE

100 g (3 & ½ oz) shelled walnuts plus more, crushed, for garnishing
1 garlic clove
100 g (⅓ cup) cooking cream
salt
grated Parmigiano Reggiano cheese

Mix the flours together on a wooden board. Add the oil and salt. Pour the water in a little at a time, working the flour with your fingertips. When the texture becomes crumbly, begin to knead with your hands. The more you knead, the more glutens will form, strengthening the pasta sheets. The movement is in the wrist: roll the pasta outwards in front of you, then fold it over onto itself and repeat the movement. When the dough is smooth, silky and no longer sticky, wrap it in plastic wrap and let rest for 30 minutes at room temperature.

Roll out the dough to large, thin sheets. Dust with semolina and let dry for about 20 minutes, until the dough is no longer sticky. Cut the pasta into 1 cm (½ inch) wide tagliatelle with the pasta machine or by hand, rolling the sheets up and cutting them with a sharp knife across intro strips.

The tagliatelle can be used immediately or wrapped into nests and dried thoroughly, then stored in a paper bag for months. Cook the pasta in boiling salted water until al dente. Drain the pasta, reserving some of the water. Prepare the sauce.

For the sauce process the walnuts with a clove of garlic, the cream, a pinch of salt and a ladle of the pasta cooking water. Dress the tagliatelle with the sauce and add a generous dusting of grated Parmigiano Reggiano and a few broken pieces of walnut.

TESTAROLI CON SUGO DI FUNGHI

Testaroli with Mushroom Sauce

from Pontremoli's Market

Testaroli are emblematic of the modest diets of upper Lunigiana. They're said to date to Roman times, when they were prepared with the same meager ingredients still used today: water, salt and flour (today wheat flour, but back then the flour would have presumably been spelt).
They take their name from *testo*, a cooking pot today made of cast iron but originally of clay. *Testaroli* are cooked in a *testo* over an open fire. This is just the first cooking phase, though. Before being ready, they are boiled in salted water, then garnished in the traditional manner with a simple pesto sauce of garlic, basil and Parmesan cheese. In lower Lunigiana the same ingredients are used to make panigacci, small, focaccia-like breads similar to testaroli but smaller. What primarily distinguishes *panigacci* is the way they are eaten: just out of the cast iron pot, accompanied by cured meats and soft cheeses, just like *tigelle* of the Emilia region of Italy.
If you want to make *testaroli* at home, mix 250 grams (2 cups) of all-purpose flour and 250 ml (1 cup & 1 tbsp) of water with a big pinch of salt. Let the batter rest at room temperature for 15 minutes. Heat a 22 cm (8 inch) non-stick pan on medium heat, then grease it with olive oil. Pour half of the batter into the hot pan and spread it gently with a spatula. Cover with a lid and cook for about 3 minutes, until it starts to dry also on the top. Flip the *testarolo* and cook for 2 minutes on the other side, then transfer to a plate. Repeat with the remaining batter. Cut the *testaroli* into lozenges, and rehydrate before dressing them as instructed in the recipe below.

INGREDIENTS FOR 4 PEOPLE

300 g (10 & ½ oz) mixed mushrooms
2 tbsp chopped parsley
1 garlic clove
2 tbsp extra virgin olive oil
200 ml (¾ cup) tomato purée
salt
red chili powder
450 g (1 lb) *testaroli*

Finely chop the garlic and parsley. Cook them in a pan with the mushrooms and olive oil for about 10 minutes, or until all the cooking liquid has evaporated. Next add the tomato purée. Adjust for salt and red chili powder, and cook for another 10 minutes, until the purée loses its raw scent.

Bring a pot of salted walter to a boil. Remove from the heat and add the *testaroli*. Rehydrate them for 3 minutes then drain and serve with the mushroom sauce.

POLENTA INCANGIATA

Polenta with Cheese

from Castelnuovo di Garfagnana's Market

My friend Annarita told me about this dish made with leftovers, common in winter. The star is a soft, velvety polenta, which is poured into a baking dish with meat ragù and Parmesan cheese and baked. Any leftovers (you must make enough to have them) are sliced and baked again with soft pecorino cheese. Its name means something like "cheese-covered polenta" (from *cacio*, an Italian word for cheese). The flour, however, is different from the usual, being more rustic and varied in color, often slightly red. Known as *formenton otto file*, this ancient Italian corn variety is cultivated primarily in Garfagnana and in the Serchio valley. Its low yield and difficult manual harvest have seen its cultivation reduced to very few farmers. Formenton otto file has a unique flavor, ensuring a tasty polenta. If you cannot find it, use any rustic corn flour for polenta. Try it with the Marovelli or other soft pecorino. I promise you will not forget this dish.

INGREDIENTS FOR 6 PEOPLE

FOR THE MEAT SAUCE
1 red onion
2 carrots
3 celery stalks
4 tbsp extra virgin olive oil
300 g (⅔ lb) ground pork
500 g (just over 1 lb) ground beef
salt
freshly ground black pepper
1 cup red wine
1.5 l (1 & ½ qt) tomato purée
2 tbsp tomato paste

FOR THE POLENTA
1.2 l (5 cups) water
1 tsp salt
300 g (10 & ½ oz) *formenton otto file* corn flour

TO ASSEMBLE THE POLENTA
8 tbsp ragù
4 tbsp grated Parmesan
4 slices of soft Tuscan pecorino cheese

Start with the meat sauce.

You can make this in advance and put some aside for the polenta, then use the rest on pastas like pici and potato-filled tortelli from Mugello (or simply keep it for the following Sunday). This recipe yields much more than what you will need for the polenta, but making a small amount isn't sensible, given the time required.

Make a fine mince of the carrots, celery and onion. Cover the bottom of a heavy bottom pot with extra virgin olive oil (while the pot is still cold) and add the vegetable mince. Cook on low heat for about 10 minutes, stirring often. The minced vegetables should start to sizzle, without burning or browning too much. Increase the heat to medium and add the ground meat. Stir with a wooden spoon, making sure the meat is broken up well and blended with the mince. Stir continuously, scraping the bottom with the spoon to incorporate all the meat. About 20 minutes are needed to cook adequately. Adjust for salt and pepper. Gradually add the red wine and reduce.

Now add the tomato purée and tomato paste, mix ing thoroughly. Lower the heat and cover the pot, leaving a small opening of the lid to allow steam to release and the sauce to simmer slowly.

Cook for at least an hour and a half, stirring occasionally.

CONTINUED ON PAGE 220

CONTINUATION OF PAGE 218

Now prepare the polenta.

Fill a large pot with 1 l of water, add the salt and bring to a boil.

Slowly pour in the flour, stirring continuously with a spoon. Lower the heat to minimum and cook for about 50 minutes, stirring often. If the polenta becomes too dense, add small amounts of water.

When the polenta is ready, oil a small rectangular baking dish.

Spread a layer of polenta into the dish. Cover the polenta with ragù and grated Parmesan. Spread another layer of polenta on top and again cover with more meat sauce and grated cheese.

You can heat the dish in the oven for about 10 minutes to melt the cheese and serve immediately.
Otherwise, keep until the next day to be prepared as follows:

Let the polenta cool and cut into vertical slices.
Put the slices back into the baking dish, alternated with slices of pecorino cheese.

Heat the oven to 200°C/400°F. Return the polenta to the oven for 15 to 20 minutes, until the cheese has melted.
Serve immediately.

TORTELLI MUGELLANI AL RAGÙ

Mugello Tortelli with Meat Sauce

from Borgo San Lorenzo's Market

Tortelli are a symbol of the culinary influences of nearby Emilia-Romagna. While the pasta is rolled out in the same manner, the filling is potato based rather than meat—an adaptation that speaks to the region's scarcity. Tortelli are served in different ways according to town, family and tradition.

INGREDIENTS FOR 6 PEOPLE

FOR THE FRESH PASTA
150 g (1 & ¼ cups) all-purpose flour
150 g (¾ cup) semolina flour
3 medium eggs
1 pinch of salt
1 tbs extra virgin olive oil

FOR THE FILLING
500 g (just over 1 lb) yellow potatoes
1 garlic clove
2 tbsp chopped parsley
1 tsp salt
½ tsp freshly ground black pepper

FOR THE MEAT SAUCE
see page 218

Combine the two flours on a wooden chopping board and shape into a mound with a large hole in the center. Crack in the eggs, add the oil and salt. Using a fork, slowly start to combine the egg and flour. When the pasta turns crumbly, switch to kneading with your hands, adding spoonfuls of cold water as needed.

Continue kneading until the glutens start to develop, as this will render the sheets of pasta stronger. The movement is all in the wrist: roll the pasta outwards in front of you, then fold it over onto itself and repeat the rolling movement. When the ball of dough is smooth, silky and no longer sticky, wrap it in plastic wrap and let rest for 30 minutes at room temperature.

Peel the potatoes and steam cook them. Let the potatoes cool and mash them. Add the parsley and chopped garlic, salt and pepper. Roll out the pasta dough to a very large, thin sheet.
Drop teaspoonfuls of the filling at regular distances from one another on each strip of pasta. Cover with another strip of pasta and, using your fingers, press the edges firmly so they are well sealed around the filling.

Cut out the tortelli using a square cutter with grooved edges. Arrange them on a platter dusted with semolina flour, making sure they do not touch and do not stick to the plate.

Bring a large, shallow pot of water to the boil. Salt the water and cook the tortelli in batches, depending on the size of the pot. They cook in just a few minutes and are ready when they rise to the water surface. Gently scoop them out and drain, then arrange in a large, high-sided platter. Serve with the sauce of your choice.
They are lovely with meat ragù or a dense game meat sauce.
These tortelli freeze well. Arrange them on a tray in one layer and then close in a freezer bag. Cook in boiling water just out of the freezer.

TOPINI DI PATATE AI FUNGHI PORCINI

Potato Gnocchi with Porcini Mushrooms

from Borgo San Lorenzo's Market

Unlike the common Italian tradition, Thursdays were never "gnocchi day" at my house. In fact, I never really liked gnocchi that much. I always found them heavy, sticky, dull. Then one day I made them at home for the first time, and I changed my mind. I prefer the smaller, round variety, the kind that in the Florentine dialect is affectionately called *topini*, or "little mice."
The best *topini* are light, pillow-soft and melt in your mouth, leaving only the flavor of the potato and just a hint of nutmeg. They are the perfect base for a sauce made from porcini mushrooms, that prized ingredient you can find at the Mugello farmers market. Ask where they have come from, and try to avoid the imported ones.
Let your nose guide you: porcini should emit a strong aroma of forest undergrowth.
An essential seasoning for mushroom sauces is *nepetella*, or calamint, a wild mint whose fresh and sharp odor is reminiscent of oregano. It grows wild throughout the Tuscan countryside and pairs well not only with mushrooms but also with artichokes and eggplant.

INGREDIENTS FOR 4–6 PEOPLE

FOR THE GNOCCHI
1 kg (2 & ¼ lb) old red potatoes
150 g (¾ cup) potato starch + more to make the gnocchi
1 egg
salt
nutmeg

FOR THE SAUCE
600 g (1 & ⅓ lb) fresh porcini mushrooms
1 garlic clove
extra virgin olive oil
salt
a few sprigs of calamint (*nepetella* or *mentuccia*)

Choose potatoes that are more or less the same size so they cook in even time. Leave them whole so they absorb less water. Rinse the potatoes under running water to remove all traces of dirt and place them in a large pot. Fill the pot with cold water and cook on medium heat until the tip of a knife easily pierces the flesh.
Drain and cool under running water.
Peel the potatoes and mash with a potato masher.
Transfer the mash to a wooden cutting board or work surface.

Using a fork, combine the potato with the beaten egg, a generous pinch of salt and a small amount of grated nutmeg.
Gradually add the starch and combine thoroughly.

Clean the work surface with a spatula. With clean hands lightly dusted with the potato starch, begin to form long links of pasta.
Cut the pasta into small cubes. Round each cube of pasta, which will be about the size of a hazelnut.

Arrange the gnocchi on a cutting board dusted with potato starch. You can cook them immediately or keep in the refrigerator for a few hours.

CONTINUED ON PAGE 227

CONTINUATION OF PAGE 224

Next make the porcini sauce.

Finely chop the garlic and cook in a pan on low heat with a few tablespoons of olive oil.
Clean the mushrooms and cut into fairly regular shapes.
When the garlic starts to sizzle, add the mushroom pieces to the pan.

Stir with a wooden spoon to flavor all the mushroom pieces.
Add a few sprigs of calamint and salt. Continue cooking on low until all the liquid cooks off and the mushrooms begin to break apart.
You should have a thick sauce.

Cook the gnocchi in plenty of salted boiling water for a few minutes, in batches if needed. They are ready when they rise to the water's surface. Scoop out with slotted spoon or ladle and transfer to the pan with the porcini sauce.

Toss the gnocchi in the sauce for 1 minute to thoroughly coat.
Add a bit of fresh calamint and serve immediately.

TORDELLI DI CAMAIORE

Camaiore Tordelli

from Camaiore's Market

Pasta fillings vary all throughout Tuscany and Italy. And what's more their names change as well: In Versilia, and especially in Camaiore, *tortelli* proudly become *tordelli*, distinguishable as well for their rich, flavorful filling. But don't be fooled by the long list of ingredients: as often happens, these *tordelli* were born as a made-over dish, prepared with the leftovers from Sunday's roast along with bread, Garfagnana pecorino, egg and thyme (called *pepolino* or *peporino* in this area). The classic sauce to serve with *tordelli* is a rich, thick meat ragù. The following recipe comes from *tordelli* experts at the Mattarello di Torcigliano restaurant in Camaiore.

INGREDIENTS FOR 6 PEOPLE

FOR THE FRESH PASTA
150 g (1 & 1/4 cups) all-purpose flour
150 g (3/4 cup) semolina
3 medium eggs
1 pinch of salt
1 tbsp extra virgin olive oil

FOR THE FILLING
400 g (14 oz) stale bread (the insides)
1 cup whole milk
200 g (7 oz) ground beef
100 g (3 & 1/2 oz) ground pork
50 g (1 & 3/4 oz) chopped mortadella
100 g (3 & 1/2 oz) chard, cooked and strained
1 small bunch fresh parsley
1 garlic clove
a few sprigs of thyme
3 tbsp aged Tuscan pecorino, grated
1 tbsp Parmesan cheese, grated
1 egg
salt
black pepper
nutmeg

FOR THE MEAT SAUCE
see page 218

Combine the two flours on a wooden work surface. Form a mound with a large hole in the middle. Crack in the eggs and add the oil and salt. Using a fork, slowly start to combine the egg and flour. When the pasta turns crumbly, switch to kneading with your hands, adding spoonfuls of cold water as needed.

Continue kneading to develop the glutens as much as possible, which strengthen the sheets of pasta. The movement is all in the wrist: roll the pasta outwards in front of you, then fold it over onto itself and repeat the movement. When the dough is smooth, silky and no longer sticky, wrap it in plastic wrap and let rest for 30 minutes at room temperature.

Next comes the fun part: making the filling.

Soak the insides of the stale bread in milk for a few minutes. Strain and transfer to a bowl. Add the ground meat and the chopped mortadella. Cut the chard into pieces and make a mince of finely chopped parsley, garlic and thyme. Add both to the mixture. Combine well and add the grated cheeses. Adjust for salt, pepper and nutmeg. Lastly add the beaten egg to help bind the filling.

After 30 minutes, roll out the pasta dough to a very large, thin sheet.

Drop teaspoonfuls of the filling at regular distances from one another on each strip of pasta.

Cover with another strip of pasta and, using your fingers, press the edges firmly so they are well sealed around the filling.

CONTINUED ON PAGE 230

CONTINUATION OF PAGE 229

Cut out the tordelli using a round cutter with grooved edges at least 5 cm in diameter (2 inches).
Arrange them on a platter dusted with semolina flour, making sure they do not touch and do not stick to the plate.

Cook the tordelli in a large, shallow pot of boiling water.
Salt the water and cook the tordelli in batches, depending on the size of the pot. Cook for a few minutes until they rise to the water surface.
Carefully remove them from the water and arrange on a large tray with high sides.
Finish in whatever way you prefer, keeping in mind that a meat ragù is certainly the best suited sauce for this pasta.

SPAGHETTI CON POMODORINI E SALSICCIA DI LARDO

Spaghetti with Cherry Tomatoes & Lardo Sausage

from the Farmers Market in Piazza Santa Caterina, Pisa

When I happened upon lardo sausage at Pisa's Santa Caterina market, I wondered how I could use it. Then I found myself buying rather a lot of it, seeing as the list of dishes that improve with a touch of lardo creamed with spices is practically endless. Sauces, frittatas, minces, toasted bread… But let's begin with spaghetti. Is there anything better than a homemade plate of spaghetti with tomato sauce? Sometimes we just want something simple and undemanding, something that fills us up and comforts with its predictability. Fresh tomato, oil and garlic: when cooked slowly and mixed with a few herbs, these simple ingredients enfold spaghetti in the flavors of summer. It's here the lardo sausage enters the scene. Dissolved in a pan with fresh tomato, it releases its sweet, rich flavor, taking tomato sauce to an entirely new level.

INGREDIENTS FOR 4 PEOPLE

80 g (3 oz) lardo sausage *
500 g (just over 1 lb) cherry tomatoes
2 garlic cloves
salt
400 g (14 oz) spaghetti
parsley

* If you cannot get to Pisa or the Biorialto di Quercianella farm, you can substitute the lardo sausage with the same amount of creamed lardo or make a mince of some lardo using a knife.

Break the sausage into pieces with your hands and place it in a non-stick pan. Wash and quarter the tomatoes. Finely chop the garlic. Add both to the pan.

Cook on low heat until the sausage is completely melted and the tomatoes have started to break apart. Adjust for salt and set aside.

Cook the spaghetti in plenty of salted boiling water. Drain 2 minutes short of being cooked, preserving a ladleful of the pasta water.

Transfer the spaghetti to the pan with the tomatoes and add some of the cooking liquid. Cook on low heat, stirring so all the liquid is absorbed. Serve immediately with a few leaves of fresh parsley.

TAGLIOLINI CACIO E PEPE COL TARTUFO

Cacio e Pepe Tagliolini with Truffle

from the White Truffle Market Fair in San Miniato

Though a traditional Roman specialty, *cacio e pepe* easily wins over we Tuscans. We often prepare this simple dish born from scarcity among migrating shepherds, who carried very few ingredients with them. In the Val d'Orcia, a classic way to make this is with pici pasta, along with a garlicky tomato sauce and fried breadcrumbs. I often make *cacio e pepe* using fresh tagliolini pasta, rather, here rendered even lovelier with a few shavings of white truffle. And here's another concession to tradition: I used Tuscan pecorino rather than Roman. Purists will disapprove, but the urge to use our own pecorino prevailed. Tagliolini with truffles is a regular feature of the San Miniato Truffle Fair and the numerous *osterie, trattorie* and restaurant menus on display all over town. Other specialties you're sure to see include white truffled eggs, truffle-seasoned cured meats and truffled beef fillets.

INGREDIENTS FOR 4 PEOPLE

FOR THE FRESH PASTA
150 g (1 & ¼ cups) all-purpose flour
150 g (¾ cup) semolina
3 medium eggs
1 pinch of salt
1 tbsp extra virgin olive oil

TO SEASON
200 g (7 oz) Tuscan pecorino
freshly ground black pepper
1 small white truffle

Combine the flours on a cutting board and shape into a mound with a large hole in the center. Break in the eggs. Add the oil and salt. Using a fork, slowly start to combine the egg and flour. When the dough turns crumbly, switch to kneading with your hands, adding spoonfuls of cold water as needed. Continue kneading to develop the glutens, which will strengthen the pasta. The movement is all in the wrist: roll the pasta outwards in front of you, then fold it over onto itself and repeat the rolling movement. When the ball of dough is smooth and silky, wrap it in plastic wrap and let rest for 30 minutes at room temperature. Roll out the pasta dough to a very large, thin sheet. Dust with semolina and let dry on the board for about 20 minutes, until the dough is no longer sticky. Cut into thin strips to make the tagliolini. Arrange the tagliolini on the cutting board so they're not touching. Form several nest shapes and dust with more semolina to prevent sticking.

Grate the pecorino into a large bowl and add the freshly ground black pepper (but not too much, otherwise it will overpower the truffle). Cook the tagliolini in salted boiling water for about 1 minute. Drain when very al dente, conserving the cooking water. Transfer the pasta to the bowl with the cheese and pepper. Add one ladleful of the pasta cooking water and combine thoroughly with a fork to form a creamy cheese and pepper sauce. Grate the truffle on top of the pasta and serve immediately before the cheese begins to stick.

TAGLIATELLE CON IL PICCIONE IN UMIDO

Tagliatelle with Stewed Pigeon

from Volterra's Market

Eating at La Carabaccia trattoria in Volterra is like eating at home, a bit like having lunch with that aunt who spends an entire morning over the stove and always serves impeccable dishes—dishes that require time and patience and that taste of home. You feel welcome here, like part of an extended family.
If it's the right time of year, try the *migliacci*, sugar-dusted crêpes made with a pork broth batter. That's right—pork broth made with pig bones and herbs. The final product bears a mere hint of pork flavor, yet even in its subtlety, it's a flavor that conjures up the traditions of our ancestors and their customary pig slaughtering.
Aside from *migliacci*, another fabulous dish here is the tagliatelle with stewed pigeon, made according to the following recipe.

INGREDIENTS FOR 4 PEOPLE

FOR THE FIRST COOKING OF THE PIGEON
2 pigeons, each weighing about 300 g (10 & ½ oz)
4 tbsp extra virgin olive oil
3 garlic cloves
a few sage leaves
½ cup vinsanto
½ cup warm water

FOR THE STEW
pigeon made prior
1 carrot
1 celery stalk
½ red onion
2 garlic cloves
a few sage leaves
2 bay leaves
4 juniper berries
2 tbsp extra virgin olive oil
1 tbsp tomato paste
600 ml (2 & ½ cups) vegetable broth
salt

Over the open stove, burn any remaining fine feathers off the pigeons' skin. Cut the pigeons into uniform pieces and place in a pan with the oil, garlic and sage leaves. Brown on medium heat for about 15 minutes.

Once the meat is browned, add the vinsanto and reduce. Add the warm water as soon as the wine has evaporated. Cook off all the liquid over low heat and let cool.

Bone the pigeons and transfer the meat on a cutting board. Pound the meat into small pieces with a knife.

Make a mince of the carrot, celery, onion, garlic, sage, bay leaves and juniper berries and put in a pan with the oil.

Cook on low heat for 5 minutes. Salt and add the chopped pigeon meat and tomato paste. Combine well to flavor. Pour in the vegetable broth and cook on low heat, stirring often, for about 40 minutes, until you have a thick and flavorful sauce similar to a meat ragù. Combine the pigeon sauce with the cooked tagliatelle and serve.

TORTELLI MAREMMANI

Maremma Style Tortelli

from the Smaller Markets in Capalbio

This was the favorite fresh pasta in my home for decades. Before Mugello *tordelli* or other pastas with seasonal fillings, before tagliolini pasta as well, these Maremma *tortelli* were the pasta dish we would have during a festivity, whether a birthday or Christmas, or any given Sunday family lunch. My grandmother made them from scratch using a grooved pasta cutter and filling them plentifully, making sure to leave a wide border around them. Then she would carry them on a large wooden tray made by my grandfather Biagio and drop them in boiling water, to cook until they rose to the water's surface. Today they are still my favorite, while my husband Tommaso continues to favor the potato-filled Mugello variety—understandably, given his Mugello origins. We meet each other halfway with the sauce: butter and sage fried until crunchy with a dusting of pecorino cheese. I found Ilena's recipe reassuring, so similar it was to my grandmother's. For years I had been eating authentic tortelli, unaware of just how much tradition that Sunday plate of pasta carried with it. Originally made with borage gathered from fields, today these tortelli are filled rather with spinach and ricotta and sometimes seasoned with marjoram.

INGREDIENTS FOR 6 PEOPLE

FOR THE FRESH PASTA
150 g (1 & ¼ cups) all-purpose flour
150 g (¾ cup) semolina
3 medium eggs
1 pinch of salt
1 tbsp extra virgin olive oil

FOR THE FILLING
650 g (1 & ½ lb) fresh spinach, thoroughly rinsed
1 garlic clove
2 tbsp extra virgin olive oil
300 g (1 & ¼ cups) ricotta
4 tbsp grated Parmigiano
salt
nutmeg

Combine the two flours on a wooden work surface. Form a mound with a large hole in the middle. Crack in the eggs and add the oil and salt. Using a fork, slowly start to combine the egg and flour.

When the pasta turns crumbly, switch to kneading with your hands, adding spoonfuls of cold water as needed. Continue kneading to develop the gluten as much as possible, which strengthen the sheets of pasta. The movement is all in the wrist: roll the pasta outwards in front of you, then fold it over onto itself and repeat the rolling movement. When the ball of dough is smooth, silky and no longer sticky, wrap it in plastic wrap and let rest for 30 minutes at room temperature.

Cook the spinach in salted boiling water for about 8 to 10 minutes. Drain and let cool then squeeze out all excess liquid. You will have about 300 grams of cooked spinach.
Chop the spinach with a knife then transfer to a pan with 1 garlic clove and a small amount of olive oil.
Cook for about 5 minutes, until the spinach has dried out and is well flavored. Next put the spinach in a bowl and combine with the ricotta. Add the grated Parmigiano and grated nutmeg. Adjust for salt.

CONTINUED ON PAGE 241

frutta

CONTINUATION OF PAGE 238

Roll the dough out to a very thin, wide, uniform sheet.
Drop teaspoonfuls of the filling at regular distances from one another along the strips of pasta. Cover with another strip of pasta and, using your fingers, press the edges firmly so they are well sealed around the filling.

Cut the tortelli with a grooved pasta cutter, leaving at least 2 fingers' worth of space around the filling.

Arrange them on a tray dusted with semolina with plenty of space between them so they do not stick.
Cook the tortelli in a large, shallow pot of salted boiling water and in batches, depending on the size of the pot.
Cook for a few minutes until the tortelli rise to the water's surface.
Carefully remove them from the water and arrange on a large tray with high sides. Season them in whatever way you prefer.

Typical favorites include a sauce of butter, sage and lots of Parmigiano or richer sauces such as meat or boar meat ragù.
I also think a light tomato sauce seasoned with a clove of garlic suits the delicate flavor of the ricotta and spinach filling.

These tortelli freeze well: arrange them on a tray in one layer and then close in a freezer bag. Cook in boiling water, just out of the freezer.

MEAT

ARISTA CON PERE E PECORINO

Roast Pork Loin with Pears and Pecorino Cheese

from Sant Ambrogio's Market in Florence

There's an old Italian adage: *Al contadino non far sapere, quanto è buono il cacio con le pere,* which means something like "Don't let the peasants find out how good cheese and pears are." It's always left me perplexed. How unlucky that the old peasant farmer couldn't have a chance to taste just-ripened pears with a slice of slightly aged pecorino (the type that still tastes of milk). In Tuscany, you see, "cheese" and "pecorino" are synonymous. For best results, choose adequately ripened pears and a not overly aged pecorino. You need enough sliced pears and cheese to cover the pork loin and "seal" it along with the prosciutto.

INGREDIENTS FOR 4 PEOPLE

800 g (1 & ¾ lb) boned pork loin
salt
freshly ground black pepper
200 g (7 oz) Tuscan prosciutto
1 ripe pear
80 g (2 & ¾ oz) medium-aged Tuscan pecorino cheese
extra virgin olive oil
200 ml (1 & ¾ cups) white wine

Rub the pork loin with salt and fresh ground pepper.

Lay sliced prosciutto on a cutting board, then arrange thin slices of peeled pear on the prosciutto, followed by thinly cut slices of pecorino.

Next place the pork loin on top. Arrange a few slices of pear and pecorino on the top of the pork loin, then wrap the prosciutto around the pork loin. Use the remaining prosciutto if needed to form a lining around the meat.

Carefully tie the pork loin with kitchen twine, making sure it is well secured and snug so it cooks evenly.

Add some oil to a cast iron pot and put it on medium heat. When the oil is hot, place the pork loin in the pot and cook on each side until the prosciutto is well browned.

Carefully turn the pork loin using two wooden spoons as to not puncture the meat and to avoid loosing any juices that keep the meat tender and flavorful.

When the meat is browned on every side, including any exposed parts that did not get covered with the prosciutto, add the white wine and reduce. Cover the pot with a lid. Let cook on medium-low heat for about 25 minutes.

Once cooked, let the pork loin rest for at least a half hour inside the pot, or wrapped in a sheet of aluminum foil, before slicing it. This way the meat's juices will set, leaving it tender and savory.

TRIPPA ALLA FIORENTINA

Florentine Tripe

from San Lorenzo Central Market in Florence

In his book *La Cucina Fiorentina* (Florentine Cuisine), Aldo Santini writes, "Tripe is the specialty dish of true Florentines, economical and excellent." For centuries, tripe vendors and their counters have brought warmth and flavor to Florence's working-class neighborhoods. Locating a recipe for Florentine tripe, however, is a challenging task, given that each family, restaurant and tripe vendor jealously guards the ingredients and measurements. Should the mince start with onion, carrot and celery? Or only onion? Or garlic? Does one use tomato purée or peeled whole tomatoes? Ask any Florentine, and he or she will swear that their family's version is the most authentic. Moving away from Florence proper, the variations only increase, with the Sienese version, for example, calling for meat sauce. Tripe is not always a favorite. In my family, however, my mother and I adore it. I've tried several different versions, each very nice. But as often happens, I've settled on what I considered the best recipe, by leaving out the extra or unnecessary ingredients.

INGREDIENTS FOR 4 PEOPLE

800 g (1 & ¾ lb) tripe
1 lemon wedge
extra virgin olive oil
1 red onion
500 g (just over 1 lb) peeled tomatoes
1 tbsp tomato paste
salt
red chili powder
grated Parmigiano Reggiano cheese
fresh bread

Ask your butcher for both the reticulum and the rumen of the tripe, as these parts have distinct textures and both are necessary to balance a well made dish of tripe.

Wash the tripe under running water. Parboil it in a large pot with a wedge of lemon for about 5 minutes. Drain and let cool. Cut the tripe into strips about 1 cm (about half an inch) wide. The strips don't need to be exactly the same, but they shouldn't be too thick.

Thinly slice the onion and sauté them in a tablespoon of oil. When they turn translucent, add the peeled tomatoes, smash them with a fork and let cook on medium heat for 15 minutes. Adjust for salt and (optional) season with red chili.

Add the tripe and the tomato paste and cook on low heat for an hour, adding small amounts of hot water occasionally if the mixture dries up. The tripe should be well seasoned and tender, with enough sauce to enjoy dipping some bread in, yet not too liquid.

Serve the tripe with plenty of fresh bread and a few spoonfuls of grated Parmigiano Reggiano cheese, if you like. Alternatively, serve the tripe in rolls which have had the soft insides removed, as you would with lampredotto. If you make sandwiches, use kaiser rolls or rosetta rolls.

LAMPREDOTTO IN ZIMINO

Lampredotto in Zimino

from San Lorenzo Central Market in Florence

I tasted *lampredotto* for the first time in Florence. It's not easy to find, actually, at either market counters nor home kitchens outside of Florence. Considered Florence's most characteristic dish, it is matched in reputation only by *bistecca alla fiorentina*, (Florentine t-bone steak) and *pappa al pomodoro*. If you are eager to spend time among true Florentines, get in line at one of the numerous tripe counters and mix with the locals, tourists, workers and students. *Lampredotto* is an institution, a rite whose phases must be properly observed. First, the roll is dipped into the *lampredotto*'s cooking juices. It can be eaten simply as is or with the addition of salt, pepper, green sauce or spicy sauce. *Lampredotto* is surprisingly delicate, despite its somewhat unconvincing appearance. How to eat *lampredotto*? Standing, while leaning slightly forward with the legs apart as to avoid dripping oil on one's clothing. If that happens, not to worry. This is the official Florentine stamp of approval. In addition to sandwiches, Florentines have come up with countless ways to enjoy *lampredotto*, from risotto to meatballs (famous at the restaurant Il Magazzino in Piazza della Passera. You can hardly tell they are made from lampredotto!). Marco and Lorella, who have a ground floor stall at the central market, advised me to try it in *zimino*, referring to a traditional Tuscan dish in which cuttlefish are cooked in a dense sauce that features leafy greens. *In zimino* requires garlic, some cherry tomatoes, plenty of herbs, chard or spinach. Not surprisingly, the origins of the term are uncertain. For some it derives from the Arabic "sàmin", meaning "herb sauce."

INGREDIENTS FOR 4 PEOPLE

500 g (just over 1 lb) lampredotto
1 carrot
1 red onion
1 celery stalk
1 small bunch fresh parsley
salt
4 tbsp extra virgin olive oil
3 garlic cloves
4 ripe datterini tomatoes
250 g (1 & ½ cups) chard, cooked and thoroughly drained of liquid
black pepper
grated Parmigiano cheese

Rinse the *lampredotto* under running water and place it in a large pot with the carrot, celery, parsley and onion. Fill the pot with water, add a generous pinch of salt and bring the liquid to a boil. Cook the lampredotto in its broth for around 45 minutes. Remove from the heat and let cool in the pot.

To make the *in zimino* sauce, first slice the *lampredotto* into thin strips.

Finely chop the garlic and brown it in olive oil in a pan, then add the *lampredotto*. Cut the tomatoes into small pieces and finely chop the chard, and add both to the pan.

Adjust the salt and pepper and let cook on high heat until the water has reduced. About 20 minutes should suffice.

Serve the *lampredotto in zimino* with large slices of bread, seasoned with additional pepper and grated Parmigiano.

PEPOSO ALLA FORNACINA CON PURÈ AL TIMO

Beef and Pepper Stew with Thyme Potato Mash

from San Lorenzo Central Market in Florence

Peposo can be made with beef shank or beef cheek. After years of tasting peposo made with beef shank, I decided to try a version made with beef cheek, per the suggestion from Marco and Lorella at San Lorenzo. Once tasted, there's no going back! The long and slow cooking renders the meat melt-in-your-mouth tender, while the veins of fat in the cut of meat used add extra flavor and tenderness (needed, given that peposo is traditionally prepared without added oil).

INGREDIENTS FOR 4 PEOPLE

FOR THE PEPOSO
800 g (1 & ¾ lb) beef cheek
5 cloves garlic, unpeeled
2 tsp black peppercorns
2 juniper berries
about 750 ml (3 cups)Chianti wine
salt

FOR THE MASH
8 large yellow potatoes
2 garlic cloves
4 tbsp extra virgin olive oill
a few sprigs of thyme
salt
black pepper
½ cup warm water

PEPOSO

Smash the pepper and juniper and enclose in a piece of gauze, forming a small pouch. In this manner the meat is seasoned during cooking, but without leaving unwelcome bits to end up in your guests' teeth.

Cut the meat into small pieces about 2 cm (¾ inch) in size. Place the meat, garlic cloves, and spice pouch in a cold pot, one with a thick bottom, preferably cast iron. Pour the red wine over the meat. Cover and cook on low heat for at least 3 hours, checking from time to time that the wine does not dry out, and adjusting for salt. If you cook the meat over low heat with the lid on, the wine should not reduce too much, but if it does, add a bit of water.

When the peposo is ready, let it rest for a while. Like all stews, its flavor will develop after a few hours. Serve warm with fresh, crusty bread, polenta, or with this potato mash.

POTATO MASH

Wash the potatoes and boil them whole, without peeling, until a fork pierces them easily. Once cooked, run them under cold water and peel. Mash them in a bowl with a fork or potato masher.

Heat the oil in a large heavy-bottom pot and add the smashed garlic and the thyme. When the garlic begins to sizzle, add the potato and half a cup warm water, and adjust for salt. Whip the potato with a whisk or with a wooden spoon until it is soft and flavored.

POLLO ARROSTO AL VINSANTO E LIMONE

Roast Chicken with Vinsanto and Lemon

from Certaldo's Market

At every market there's at least one rotisserie serving roasted meats like spitfire chickens. Their enticing aromas catch your attention from afar, drawing you towards the array of meats and croquettes. My grandfather Biagio would take me to the rotisserie every Friday morning to pick up roasted potatoes, and my grandmother and I continue the tradition of an obligatory visit whenever we go to market. Occasionally I stop there on my own as well, but when I can't, I follow this recipe of mine to immediately recreate the feeling of Sunday lunch with the family.

INGREDIENTS FOR 4 PEOPLE

1 chicken weighing approximately 1.5 kg (3 & ⅓ lb)
1 organic lemon (not chemically treated)
2 tsp fine salt
2 tsp black peppercorns
50 ml (¼ cup) extra virgin olive oil
1 small glass of vinsanto

Heat the oven to 210°C/410°F.

Crush the pepper in a mortar until it's reduced to a powder. Mix in the salt and use this mix to rub down the chicken. Then rub the chicken with olive oil and 2 spoonfuls of vinsanto. Pierce the lemon a few times with a fork and insert it inside the chicken.

Pour 60 ml of vinsanto into a baking dish. Place the chicken in the dish, breasts facing up.

Roast the chicken for about 30 minutes, then turn it so the breasts are facing down. Baste with the remaining vinsanto. Lower the heat to 180°C/355°F and continue cooking for another 30 to 40 minutes, until the chicken is golden on all sides.

Wrap the chicken in aluminum foil and let rest for at least a half hour. Serve with the pan juices.

FAGIOLI ALL'UCCELLETTO

Tuscan White Beans with Sausage

from Arezzo's Market

This is perhaps one of the most iconic recipes of the region: beans and sausages, popular ingredients in Tuscan cuisine, are cooked together over low heat until the beans turn creamy and the sausages release their fats and flavor. You'll find this dish in nearly every trattoria throughout Tuscany, either as a hearty side or main course. The name comes to us from Pellegrino Artusi, who noted that these beans were prepared with the same seasonings used to cook *uccellini*, or small birds—namely sage and garlic. The recipe below calls for *sambudello*, a dark red sausage made from the most economic (and reddest) parts of the pig, ground together with the liver, heart, tongue, cheek and *rigatino* (similar to pancetta). *Sambudello*'s texture is soft, with a spicy flavor owing to large doses of salt, pepper, garlic and fennel. Today *sambudello* is prepared like any traditional sausage, either fresh or grilled, served with plenty of good Tuscan bread. In times past, people in the Casentino area would have eaten it with a polenta made from roasted chestnuts. If you have trouble finding *sambudello*, use fresh sausages.

INGREDIENTS FOR 4 PEOPLE

600 g (3 & ⅓ cups) cooked cannellini beans (or other white bean)
extra virgin olive oil
1 garlic clove
sage leaves
2 tbsp tomato paste
salt
black pepper
4 sambudello sausages

Heat a few tablespoons of extra virgin olive oil in a large, deep pot and add an unpeeled garlic clove and a few sage leaves. When the garlic has seasoned the oil and the sage begins to turn color, remove the garlic and pour in the whole beans along with a few ladles of their cooking liquid. Add the tomato paste to color the beans and let simmer on low to allow the flavors to combine. Adjust for salt and pepper.

Simmer on low for about 20 minutes. Remove the casings from the sausages and add to the beans. Continue until the meat is completely cooked.

Serve hot, with toasted Tuscan bread to sop up the juices.

ARISTA IN PORCHETTA

Roast Pork with Tuscan Herbs

from Arezzo's Market

Livorno is known for its chickpea pancakes, Florence for its lampredotto sandwiches. And Arezzo? Arezzo has several specialties, but the one you simply cannot miss is *porchetta*. *Porchetta* sandwiches are the star among street foods at any fair or market, with good reason. The people of Arezzo love their *porchetta*, wholly and unconditionally, whether in a sandwich or on its own. Making an entire *porchetta* roast at home can be quite a challenge, though. This roast recipe, anyway, is suited to home ovens and Sunday family gatherings—a worthy substitute for the traditional Tuscan roasted pork loin. It doesn't leave out the crunchy skin wrapping, either, my favorite part of the classic sandwich, too!

INGREDIENTS FOR 8 PEOPLE

a few sprigs rosemary
a few sage leaves
2 garlic cloves
2 tsp fine salt
1 tsp freshly ground black pepper
650 g (1 & ½ lb) boned pork loin
500 g (just over 1 lb) thick pancetta (1 cm/0.5 inches) with the skin
extra virgin olive oil
500 g (just over 1 lb) nouvelle potatoes

Start by preparing a mince of the garlic, sage and rosemary, the holy trinity of Tuscan cuisine. Combine with salt and pepper to obtain a classic blend used to season every Tuscan roast, whether meat or fish.

Place the pork loin on a cutting board and rub it down with the seasoning, leaving some aside for the potatoes.

Wrap the loin tightly with the pancetta (the "skin") and secure it firmly with butcher's twine.

Place the pork loin in a baking dish and moisten with olive oil. Arrange the unpeeled potatoes around the meat. Season the potatoes with a drizzle of olive oil and some of the seasoning.

Heat the oven to 200°C/400°F and cook for about 75 minutes, basting the pancetta from time to time with the pan juices.

The pork loin will be moist and flavorful thanks to the spiced salt rub and the pancetta seal, while the skin will become crisp just as a pork roast should.

Let rest outside the oven for at least 20 minutes before slicing and serving. It can also be eaten cold, sliced thinly as you would for a porchetta sandwich.

POLLO IN UMIDO CON ROCCHINI DI SEDANO

Stewed Chicken with Celery Croquettes

from Montevarchi, the First Earth Market

I heard about this dish for the first time while visiting a country house called La Selva Giardino del Belvedere, tucked away in the woods outside Montevarchi. The house seemed like something out of a mid-winter's dream: fireplaces, wood-fired ovens, two kitchens, marble and wooden counters, bookshelves, candles, and shrubbery, berries and flowers. We were there organizing a Christmas party, but, as often happens, I began to wander around and ended up talking about local recipes. Later on, I found this recipe in Guido Gianni's book *La Cucina Aretina* (The Cuisine of Arezzo). This hearty "working man's" dish is often prepared using Valdarno chicken, a source of great pride to local producers.

INGREDIENTS FOR 4 PEOPLE

FOR THE CHICKEN STEW
1 red onion
1 celery stalk
1 carrot
2 garlic cloves
1 small bunch fresh parsley
a few basil leaves
a few sprigs of thyme
3 tbsp extra virgin olive oil
½ chicken, cleaned and pieced
salt
freshly ground black pepper
½ cup red wine
1 cup tomato purée

FOR CELERY CROQUETTES
300 g (10 & ½ oz) celery
100 g (¾ cup) all-purpose flour
1 egg, beaten
salt
grated Parmigiano Reggiano cheese
oil for frying

Make a mince with onion, celery, parsley, carrot and garlic along with basil and thyme. Add a few tablespoons of olive oil to an earthenware crock pot with a thick bottom. Brown the mince on low heat for a few minutes. When the mince is softened, add the chicken pieces and brown on medium heat. If the pot is too small, brown few chicken pieces at a time to make sure each piece is well browned on all sides. Adjust for salt and pepper.

Add the red wine and reduce. Add the tomato purée. Turn the chicken pieces so each is covered with the purée, lower the heat and cook uncovered. Add small amounts of water as needed to keep the chicken from sticking. It's ready after about 30 minutes.

Make the celery croquettes in the meantime.

Remove the celery strings, rinse and cut into 10-cm (4 inches) pieces. Cook the celery in boiling salted water for 30 minutes or until tender. Drain and let cool. Using your hands, thoroughly press out all excess liquid. You will have a mushy mound.

Form small balls with the celery. Flour them and dip in the egg. Then repeat the process: flour and egg the balls one more time. Fry the croquettes in plenty of hot oil for about 5 minutes, turning them constantly until they turn golden.

Remove the chicken from the sauce and arrange on a serving tray. Transfer the croquettes to the sauce and turn so each is covered. Serve the croquettes as a side dish to the chicken, with a dusting of grated Parmigiano Reggiano cheese.

AGNELLO FRITTO CON I CARCIOFI

Fried Lamb with Artichokes

from Pontremoli's Market

Among the Slow Food presidia of Lunigiana, alongside Pontremoli *testaroli* and Marocca di Casola bread, there is also an indigenous sheep breed that has lived in this area since time immemorial, the *Zaresca*. Thanks to the isolation of Lunigiana, the Zerasca sheep breed has managed to maintain its characteristics unaltered over time. The animals are kept indoors only during the coldest months, and spend the rest of the year being pastured. The Zeri lambs have a tender and fragrant meat, due to a diet consisting essentially of mother's milk and organic pasture. Traditionally it is cooked *al testo*, flavored with a mixture of minced lard, garlic, parsley, rosemary and sage and accompanied by local potatoes. When I asked my grandmother how she would prepare the lamb, she asked if I also had artichokes. To my affirmative answer, her reaction was immediate: 'Fry it, with artichokes!'

INGREDIENTS FOR 4 PEOPLE

800 g (about 1 ¾ lb or 12 pieces) lamb chops
4 artichokes
4 eggs
200 g (1 & ⅔ cups) all-purpose flour
200 g (2 & ⅓) homemade breadcrumbs or panko
fine sea salt
lemon thyme sprigs
vegetable oil for frying
lemon, to serve

In a medium bowl, beat the eggs with a generous pinch of salt.

Prepare two plates, one with flour and a pinch of salt, the other with breadcrumbs, thyme leaves, and salt.

Coat the lamb ribs with flour, dip them in the beaten eggs, then coat them again in the breadcrumbs. Dip them again in the eggs and eventually coat them with breadcrumbs, then place them on a tray.

Clean the artichokes: remove the tougher outer leaves, cut them into quarters and rub them with lemon juice so that they do not turn black. Dip them first in flour, then in the beaten eggs and finally in breadcrumbs and place them on the tray.

Fry the lamb chops in plenty of hot oil until golden brown, about three minutes per side, and then the artichokes, also until golden brown.

Serve the lamb and artichokes hot, sprinkled with salt and thyme, accompanied by a few lemon wedges.

SPEZZATINO ALLA BIRRA

Beef and Beer Stew

from Castelnuovo di Garfagnana's Market

A craft beer trend has been brewing across Italy recently. One fascinating aspect of the microbrewery movement here is the link between master beer makers and the products characteristic of their area. The brewery La Petrognola is one example, producing white, amber and dark farro beers, the double malt farro beer "Sandy" and the chestnut beer "Marron"—all of which reflect this land.

INGREDIENTS FOR 6 PEOPLE

1 red onion
extra virgin olive oil
3 tbsp flour
salt
freshly ground black pepper
1.2 kg (2 & ⅔ lb) stew beef
330 ml dark farro beer
4 medium carrots
1 celery stalk
400 g (14 oz) potatoes
1 bay leaf
1 sprig rosemary
400 ml (1 & ⅔ cups) light vegetable broth

Finely slice the onion and cook in a few tablespoons of extra virgin olive oil for about 5 minutes, adding very small amounts of water to prevent the onions from browning too much. Meanwhile, lightly oil the pieces of stew beef. Mix a generous pinch of salt and a grinding of black pepper with the flour. Flour the meat and then shake well to remove the excess. Add the meat to the pot and brown well, adding a few drops of oil if needed. Cook the meat on high heat for 2 to 3 minutes, making sure to sear all sides.

Pour in the beer and let reduce for about 5 minutes over medium-low heat. Slice the carrots and celery into thin rounds. Cube the potatoes. Add the vegetables to the pot along with a pinch of salt, the bay leaf and the rosemary. Pour the vegetable broth over the meat and vegetables. Mix well and cook on low heat, covered, for at least two hours, checking from time to time that the cooking liquid doesn't completely dry out. If more liquid is needed to finish cooking the meat, add more broth. If instead there's too much liquid, turn the heat up and let thicken.

The meat should be tender enough to cut with a fork, and the sauce should be thick and flavorful.

POLLO IN CAMICIA NERA DI MARIA

Maria's "Black-Shirted" Chicken

from Montecatini Earth Market

Among the many recipes Maria and I discussed was this recipe for chicken dressed in "black shirts," a quirky reference to Italy's Fascist era inspired by the dark sauce of black olives and red wine. (In some rural areas, red wine used to be called black wine, as a simple distinction from white.)
This slow-cooked chicken has a flavorful sauce thanks to the olives and a mince, and it's finished with a pesto of raw garlic and rosemary for a final burst of color and robust flavor.
Though not for the faint of palate, this chicken dish is well suited to Sunday lunches in the countryside, ideally served with plenty of fresh bread to dip in the sauce.

INGREDIENTS FOR 4 PEOPLE

1 whole chicken, cleaned and skinned, approximately 1.2 kg (2 & ⅔ lb)
150 g (5 oz) blacked olives, pitted
1 celery stalk
1 carrot
½ red onion
extra virgin olive oil
1 cup red wine
salt
black pepper
2 sprigs rosemary
2 garlic cloves

Rinse the chicken under running water and cut into even pieces.

Chop and crush the black olives and set aside.

Make a mince of the celery, carrot and onion. In a large pan with a few tablespoons of olive oil, cook the mince until it just starts to sizzle and soften, about 5 minutes.

Now add the chicken pieces and brown on all sides on medium heat. If the pan isn't large enough to accommodate all the pieces at once, work in batches, resting the browned pieces on a plate as you proceed.

When all the chicken pieces are well browned, return them to the pan and pour in a cup of red wine. Increase the heat and reduce.

Add the black olive pesto and adjust for salt and pepper. Cover the chicken with a cup of hot water and combine well to thoroughly coat each piece of meat with the olive mixture. Lower the heat. Cover and cook on low until all the liquid evaporates. Make sure the chicken is completely cooked. Add ladlefuls of water as needed to finish the cooking.

Finely chop the rosemary sprigs together with the garlic. Serve the chicken warm, dusted with the rosemary and garlic mixture.

LONZA

Beef Cheek and Lip Stew

from Borgo San Lorenzo's Market

In the Mugello and other areas around Florence, *lonza* does not only mean loin but is also the name of a stew, one made from beef cuts like cheek and lips–an economic yet very flavorful dish. These cuts, the ones that tend to get tossed out, require patience and longer cooking times, but can be quite satisfying. When I asked my butcher for beef cheek and lips, he gave me a look of pride, as if he'd spotted a kindred spirit. Then he burst into laughter: "Oh, today Giulia is making something good," he said to the others in line with me.

INGREDIENTS FOR 4–6 PEOPLE

1 kg (2 & ¼ lb) of beef cheek and lip pieces
extra virgin olive oil
salt
black pepper
red chili powder
1 cup red wine
1 garlic clove
1 red onion
1 small bunch fresh parsley
1 clove
½ tsp nutmeg
½ tsp cinnamon
½ l (2 cups) warm water
2 tbsp tomato paste

Cut the lip and cheek into pieces. Season with salt, pepper and a pinch of chili powder. Brown the meat for about 10 minutes in a few tablespoons of oil until well browned on all sides. Pour in the red wine and let reduce completely. Make a mince of the garlic, onion and parsley and add it to the meat. Grind the clove and mix it with the cinnamon and nutmeg. Add the spices to the meat.

Add the tomato paste to the warm water, dissolve, and pour into the pot. Cover and cook for at least 2 and ½ hours, adding more water as needed should the stew dry out.

Serve the *lonza* with a good red wine and plenty of fresh bread for dipping in the sauces.

CINGHIALE ALLA MAREMMANA

Maremma Style Wild Boar

from the Smaller Markets in Capalbio

The Maremma has long been a hunting and game area, going back to the time of the Etruscans, who would lure animals into their nets by playing double flutes. Wild boar is likely the most recognized and emblematic animal known to this region, a symbol of the Natural Park of Maremma and the L'Uccellina, a stretch of wild, pure land with hills covered in Mediterranean maquis—humid and full of marshlands and swamps, as well as pine groves, sandy beaches, dunes and sea cliffs. The boar also plays a role in mysterious local legends, figuring as a kind of mythical creature of ever-larger size capable of winning the esteem of the hunters who seek to capture him.

Wild boar is also the star of the countless food festivals that light up inland and coastal Maremma in summer and fall. This recipe for Maremma style boar is from Ilena, who suggests not marinating the meat, as this strips the meat of its gamey flavor, along with that mythical quality which rendered it for so long the center of fireside tales. The walnut added during cooking seems to help absorb that hint of wildness that remains, making it palatable to everyone.

INGREDIENTS FOR 4 PEOPLE

800 g (1 & ¾ lb) boned boar meat
extra virgin olive oil
2 garlic cloves
4 bay leaves
2 sprigs rosemary
dried chili pepper
½ cup red wine vinegar
1 cup red wine
500 g (just over 1 lb) peeled tomatoes
200 ml (¾ cup) tepid water
1 walnut
salt

Break the boar meat into pieces roughly the size of a walnut.

Cover the bottom of a large pot with olive oil. Add the garlic cloves, the bay leaves, the rosemary and chili pepper. Heat on medium and brown the meat for about 10 minutes, until all sides are browned.

Pour the vinegar over the meat and reduce. Add the red wine and cook off the liquid on low heat. This will take about 20 to 25 minutes.

Break up the tomatoes and add to the pot along with the water. Add the walnut. Adjust for salt and cook slowly on very low heat for at least 1 and ½ hours, adding additional water as needed. You should have a thick sauce, and the boar meat should be tender.

Serve as a main course or as a sauce for tagliatelle, accompanied by a nice grating of pecorino cheese.

SCOTTIGLIA MAREMMANA

Maremma Style Mixed Meat Stew

from the Indoor Market in Grosseto

The uncertain origins of this stew read like a classic case of "the chicken and the egg."
It was certainly known to the Casentino woodsmen who every year would head to the Maremma to make their charcoal. So could they have brought this dish with them and shared the recipe with Maremma housewives? Or was it the opposite? Did the dish originate with Maremma people, and did they share it with their Casentino guests who in turn took it back with them to their forests?
One thing we can say with certainty about *scottiglia*—it is a nourishing and invigorating stew suited to outdoor laborers. It also bears that same irreverent and witty spirit found in *cacciucco*. Both combine ingredients on hand that need to be used up to prevent waste: in the case of *cacciucco*, this means bony, economic fish, and with *scottiglia*, meats of every kind, from chicken and guinea fowl to rabbit, lamb, pork, boar and pheasant—plus anything else hunters may have trapped.
Traditionally, *scottiglia* would have been cooked in large pots in the outdoors, flavored with whatever herbs were available nearby and served with a hearty wine. This version from Ilena, though refined, maintains a discernible touch of the Maremma.

INGREDIENTS FOR 6–8 PEOPLE

extra virgin olive oil
4 garlic cloves
500 g (just over 1 lb) rabbit meat, pieced
500 g (just over 1 lb) chicken meat, pieced
500 g (just over 1 lb) guinea fowl meat, pieced
salt
dried chili pepper
about 20 sage leaves
2 sprigs rosemary
1 cup white wine

Cook the garlic in the oil, then add the meat and brown thoroughly on all sides for about 10 minutes. Work in batches if the pot is not large enough, browning a few pieces at a time so they cook uniformly.

Return all the meat to the pot together, salt and add the sage, rosemary and red chili (according to your taste).

Pour in the white wine and cook on low heat until all the wine is cooked off.

At this point, the *scottiglia* stew is ready.

FISH

STOCCAFISSO ALLA VOLTERRANA

Volterra Style Stockfish

from Volterra's Market

On a clear day, you can see the sea from Volterra. First you smell it in the air, on those windy days that bring a breeze from the coasts to the east. The sea-salty air blends with the smell of maritime pine trees. Climb upwards towards Piazza Martiri della Libertà, turn to face the Balze hills, and in the distance you'll glimpse the shimmery stretch of sea on the horizon.

You can also experience the sea, albeit in a different way, at Pescheria del Peschereccio fish shop, which benefits from the proximity of the coast and offers fresh fish daily. This recipe comes directly from Beatrice at the fish shop, who was very precise in her quantities, methods and tricks.

The stockfish cream absorbs the flavors of the tomato and onion, becoming a tasty spread to use on toasted bread as a starter or snack, as a pasta sauce or a base for any fish pasta.

INGREDIENTS FOR 8 PEOPLE

800 g (1 & ¾ lb) pink onions
extra virgin olive oil
dried chili pepper
500 g (just over 1 lb) stockfish, already soaked
1 kg (2 & ¼ lb) peeled tomatoes
salt

Peel and thinly slice the onions. Place them in a large pan with a few tablespoons of oil and a pinch of dried chili. Cook on low until the onions start to soften.

Cut the stockfish into pieces and break up the tomatoes with your hands. Add both to the pan. Cook for at least 2 hours, stirring periodically, adding small amounts of water as needed should the mixture dry out. Adjust for salt at the end. You should have a thick sauce, almost like a mousse, that you can spread on bread or use as a base for lots of other recipes.

ACCIUGHE FRITTE

Fried Anchovies

from the Central Food Market in Livorno

Talking with Maruska of the Mare Blu fish shop is as educational as it is fun—she simply floors you. I met up with her while she was cleaning anchovies, opening them and arranging them on the fish stand. "What are you doing here at this hour?" she asked. "I suppose you know that to get the best fish available you have to get here early, as soon as the market opens? Otherwise you should get here a little before closing, to get the best deals." She immediately puts you in your place. Then she generously rewards you with her years of experience, her recipes, her knowledge gained from many long, early hours spent cleaning fish, her surgeon-like precision and pianist's grace.

"Anchovies should not be eaten raw," she says, "as they can be dangerous. And if I tell you that these can be marinated in oil and vinegar and then covered with a pesto of parsley and garlic, well, you should trust me. I can also tell you where these were fished, when, and by whom. In any case, these fish are meant to be fried." And then she told me how to fry them, according to her simple and straightforward method.

INGREDIENTS FOR 4 PEOPLE

500 g (just over 1 lb) very fresh anchovies
1 egg
salt
pepper
150 g (1 & ⅓ cups) breadcrumbs
500 ml (2 & ⅓ cups) quality seed oil
1 lemon

Clean the anchovies by removing the guts, head and bones. Open them and quickly rinse under water.

Beat the egg with a pinch of salt and a pinch of pepper. Dip the anchovy into the just beaten egg and then into the breadcrumbs, pressing them well to make sure the breadcrumbs stick.

Heat the oil in a (not too wide) pan. Fry the anchovies in the oil for a few minutes on each side, until golden. Fry them in batches so they cook evenly without breaking.

Scoop them out and drain off the excess oil. Transfer to a plate covered with paper towels as you proceed with the remaining fish.

Season with salt and fresh squeezed lemon juice and serve.

IL BACCALÀ
Salted Codfish

In response to my queries about traditional recipes as I travelled around Tuscany's markets, often the name of a certain ingredient would come out, an ingredient that has shaped the history of poor diets among countless Italians: Baccalà, or codfish.
Some of the most popular ways of making cod in Italy are the Florentine or Livornese style (fried then cooked in tomato), in a sweet and sour sauce with raisins and pine nuts, boiled with chickpeas as done in the Pistoia area, or with leeks as they do in Versilia.

Salt cod enjoys a good reputation in Florence, and deservedly so, because the Florentines know how to soften it well, cleaning it frequently with a little hard brush. Moreover, the cod consumed in Florence is usually the best Labrador cod, which is fatty by nature and relatively tender, considering the tough, fibrous flesh of this type of fish, which is not suited to weak stomachs. For this reason, I have never been able to digest it.
Pellegrino Artusi, *Science in the Kitchen and the Art of Eating Well*

Cod has played a fundamental role in nourishing Italians, including we Tuscans. It's a traditional dish served on so-called lean days. When my grandmother was young here in inland Tuscany, cod was the only fish consumed, and regularly so, every Friday.

TAGLIOLINI PORRI E BACCALÀ

Tagliolini with Leeks and Codfish

from the Farmers Market at the Ancient Forum Boarium in Lucca

It was at Trattoria Canuleia in Lucca, seated in the garden on a beautiful summer evening, where I tried tagliolini with leeks and cod.
The pasta and leeks blend well together, the leeks having been cooked prior in a pan to form a flavorful sauce. The white, firm fish is added at the end to lend a traditional touch to this simple, wholesome recipe.

INGREDIENTS FOR 4 PEOPLE

FOR THE FRESH PASTA
150 g (1 & ¼ cups) all-purpose flour
150 g (¾ cup) semolina
3 medium eggs
1 pinch of salt
1 tbsp extra virgin olive oil

FOR THE SAUCE
2 medium leeks
4 tbsp extra virgin olive oil
450 g (1 lb) codfish, previously soaked
black pepper
1 pinch of salt

Combine the two flours on a cutting board and shape into a mound with a large hole in the center. Crack in the eggs and add the oil and salt. Using a fork, slowly start to combine the egg and flour. When the pasta turns crumbly, switch to kneading with your hands, adding spoonfuls of cold water as needed. Continue kneading until the glutens start to develop, as this will render the sheets of pasta stronger. The movement is all in the wrist: roll the pasta outwards in front of you, then fold it over onto itself and repeat the rolling movement.

When the ball of dough is smooth, silky and no longer sticky, wrap it in plastic wrap and let rest for 30 minutes at room temperature.

Roll out the pasta dough to a very large, thin sheet. Dust with semolina and let dry on the board for about 20 minutes, until the dough is no longer sticky. Cut into thin strips to make the tagliolini. Arrange the tagliolini on the cutting board so they're not touching. Form several nest shapes and dust with more semolina to dry them quickly.

Next make the leek and cod sauce. Thinly slice the leeks up to their green parts. Place the sliced leeks in a large pot with extra virgin olive oil and a pinch of salt. Cover and cook on medium-low for about 20 minutes. Halfway through the cooking time add 2 tbsp of hot water to prevent burning.

In the meantime, boil the cod in a pot for about 10 minutes on medium heat. Drain and break the fish into pieces with a fork.
Add the fish to the leeks and cook for a few minutes more to flavor. Remove from the heat and set aside. Cook the tagliolini in salted boiling water for about 1 minute. Drain when the pasta is still al dente and transfer to the pan with the sauce along with a few spoonfuls of the hot pasta water. Toss well with a large fork, dust with black pepper and serve immediately.

PASTA ALLA TRABACCOLARA

Pasta with Mixed Fish and Tomatoes

from the Fish Market on the Pier of Viareggio

This dish takes its name from *trabaccolo*, a kind of vessel used by the fishermen of San Benedetto del Tronto. The name is a bit misleading, however, given that the dish is as much a piece of Viareggio tradition as is Carnival.

In the period between the two world wars, many fishing families from San Benedetto del Tronto left the Adriatic. Compelled by poverty and losses resulting from World War I, they moved to Viareggio, where some of their fellow citizens had already set up a colony in the late 19th century.

Trabaccolara is a poorman's dish, made with the demersal fish unsold at market. This sauce traditionally accompanies large bowls of spaghetti or linguine, but you can also use hollow short rod pasta like *paccheri* or *mezze maniche* for a nice result: the flavors of the sea mixed with tomato fill up the pasta to lovely effect.

INGREDIENTS FOR 4 PEOPLE

FOR THE FISH FUMET

- bones from the fish used for the sauce
- 1 basil leaf
- 2 cherry tomatoes
- 1 tsp salt

FOR THE SAUCE

- 300 g (10 & ½ oz) fish fillets (mullet, rockfish, striped seabream, gurnard, weever fish...)
- 2 whites of spring onions
- 1 piece dried chili pepper
- 100 g (3 & ½ oz) cherry tomatoes
- zest of ½ an organic lemon
- a few basil leaves
- extra virgin olive oil
- ½ cup white wine
- 400 g (14 oz) *mezze maniche, paccheri* or similar pasta

Ask your fishmonger to fillet the fish for you, or do this yourself if you're able. Save the fish carcass. Add the fish bones to a pot with 2 l of water. Cut the tomatoes in half and add to the water along with the basil leaf and a teaspoon of salt. Cook on low heat for about 1 hour. Filter the liquid and top up with more fresh water to cook the pasta in.

Make the sauce while the pasta is cooking.

Quarter the tomatoes. Finely slice the onions. Add both to a large pan together with a piece of dried chili and the lemon zest. Tear in some basil leaves. Add a small amount of oil and cook on low for 7 to 8 minutes, until the tomatoes are just coming apart. Next add the wine, raise the heat and reduce. Add the fish and cook until tender enough to break with a fork. Remove from the heat and set aside.

Drain the pasta 2 minutes before done: it will finish cooking in the saucepan. Add the cooked pasta to the pan along with 2 ladlefuls of the pasta water. Combine thoroughly over medium heat until ready (similar to risotto). The starch from the pasta will form a thick sauce with the fish and tomatoes. Serve immediately.

CARBONARA DI ARSELLE

Arsella Clam Carbonara

from the Central Food Market in Livorno

Stand number 160 at the Livorno market sells eggs, and not just any eggs but all manner of very special eggs, including Livornese hen eggs, eggs for drinking, eggs from Lari, free range hen eggs, and eggs of different sizes and colors, from pink to white. Also on offer are Parisi eggs, available only in Livorno.
Paolo Parisi lives in a small farm house in Usigliano near Lari, in the Pisan countryside. He started off making Cinta Senese salami, then later goose salamis. Now his farm raises Livornese hens and produces some of the best eggs in Italy, popular with chefs and high-end restaurants. What makes these eggs so special? Parisi feeds his hens on goat's milk, obtaining eggs very white in color, with soft, fatty yolks and rich whites.
"And how should they be used?" I asked the gentleman at the Parisi stand. The answer was: "In a carbonara sauce, but with clams."
Of course I'd heard of many variations on the classic Italian carbonara, those calling for zucchini or asparagus, for instance. But it had never occurred to me to substitute the guanciale with arsella clams (carpet shell clams in English). If you are able to get your hands on some of these small coastal clams harvested from clean, calm seas, definitely try this recipe. They're not easy to find, so you can use other types of clams as long as they are small. The rich egg yolk renders the spaghetti silky, while the clams give the pasta a lovely sea flavor.

INGREDIENTS FOR 4 PEOPLE

400 g (14 oz) arsella clams or similar
1 garlic clove
¼ cup white wine
extra virgin olive oil
4 egg yolks
500 g (just over 1 lb) spaghetti
1 small bunch fresh parsley
freshly ground black pepper

Soak the clams in a bowl of water for an hour to remove the sand. Drain thoroughly.

Add some oil to a large pan. Smash the garlic clove and add to the pan. Heat until the garlic flavors the oil. Add the clams and stir. Add the white wine and reduce. As soon as the wine has evaporated, cover the pan with a lid. Cook on medium heat for a few minutes, shaking the pan from time to time until the clams open. Set aside.

Cook the spaghetti in plenty of salted water, following the package instructions. Meanwhile, place the egg yolks in a bowl and add a spoonful of the pasta water.

When the spaghetti is cooked, drain and transfer to the pan with the clams.

Now add the egg yolks and stir well. The heat of the spaghetti and clams will work on the yolks to create a rich, creamy sauce.

Garnish with chopped fresh parsley and a bit of freshly ground black pepper. Serve immediately.

PENNE CON ZUCCHINE E BOTTARGA DI ORBETELLO

Penne with Zucchini and Orbetello Bottarga

from the Market of Orbetello by the Sea

Walking along the quay at Orbetello's lagoon where the Saturday morning market is held, I was struck by the enchanting scene, one rarely witnessed for those, like me, accustomed to markets in inland or hilly places. A stack of crates containing small, light green zucchini caught my eye, set against the sea backdrop so blue it could be taken for the sky.
The sea aroma in the air blended with the earthy, green scent of the zucchini, bringing to mind a dish like a spark igniting my imagination.
I'd seen this dish before, the evening we went to dinner at I Pescatori di Orbetello, where the black on white sign for pasta with zucchini and Orbetello bottarga grabbed my attention. You could order it right there at the stand and enjoy your meal with a view of the lagoon.

INGREDIENTS FOR 4 PEOPLE

8 medium zucchini, light green
2 garlic cloves
8 datterini tomatoes (or similar)
about 10 basil leaves + more for garnishing
extra virgin olive oil
salt
freshly ground black pepper
350 g (12 oz) penne pasta
50 g (1 & ¾ oz) Orbetello mullet bottarga

Rinse the zucchini, slice off the ends and cut into thin strips. Smash the garlic cloves and place in a large pan with a few tablespoons of extra virgin olive oil. Quarter the tomatoes and add to the pan along with the zucchini. Tear in the basil leaves.

Cook on medium heat for about 15 minutes, stirring often, until the zucchini are soft but still somewhat al dente.

Adjust for salt and pepper.

Meanwhile, cook the pasta in plenty of salted boiling water. Set aside some of the cooking water before draining the pasta. Add the pasta to the pan along with a ladleful of cooking water.

Briskly toss the pasta on high heat for 1 minute to distribute the sauce.

Just before serving, grate the bottarga on the pasta, stirring one last time. Serve with the remaining fresh basil.

CACIUCCO

Livornese Fish Stew

from the Central Food Market in Livorno

Like all soups, Livornese *cacciucco* is highly influenced by seasonality and the use of leftovers. For this reason, it's not easy to pinpoint a definitive recipe for *cacciucco*, which is made from the smallest and least valuable fish left over on the fishing boat or unsold at fish counters. There are, however, a few rules to follow when choosing the ingredients for *cacciucco*.
Garlic and sage are fundamental, not only for the extra flavor they add but also for their disinfectant properties. The tomato paste has its role as well, being a more economical and practical way to take tomato on board of a ship, rather than pounds of fresh tomato. And the red chili, a favorite of the Livornese, is always included. Regarding the choice of fish, don't bother with more select types like prawns or mussels. Choose bony fish, those typically considered less desirable yet full of flavor. Equip yourself with a bit of patience and invite others to lunch. As Maruska says, *cacciucco* is not a dish to be eaten alone but rather one that brings together friends in warmth and comfort. The following version is hers, yet as many versions of this soup exist as there are kitchens in Livorno, if not more.

INGREDIENTS FOR 4 PEOPLE

extra virgin olive oil
2 garlic cloves
a few sage leaves
red chili powder
50 g (1 & ¾ oz) tomato paste
1 ladleful fish stock
or hot water
½ cup red wine
500 g (just over 1 lb) baby octopus,
cleaned and sliced into thin strips
500 g (just over 1 lb) cuttlefish,
cleaned and sliced
into thin strips
400 g (14 oz) small smooth hounds
400 g (14 oz) mixed fish
with the bones still in
(gurnard, rockfish, lesser weever...)
8 mantis shrimps
salt
4 slices bread

Chop the garlic. Cover the bottom of a pot with oil and cook the garlic, sage and chili pepper. Add the baby octopus and cook on low heat for about 15 minutes. Add the cuttlefish and cook for a few minutes more. Dissolve the tomato paste in a small amount of warm water or fish stock and add. Pour in the wine.

Cook for about 20 minutes on medium-low heat. Stir often to make sure the soup doesn't stick to the pot. Should it dry out too much, add another ladleful of fish stock. Adjust for salt as needed.

Next add the fish with bones and the smooth hounds, arranging them on top of the soup so they steam. Finish with the mantis shrimp and cook the soup for another 10 minutes, covered.

Serve in individual bowls with a slice of grilled bread at the bottom, which can be smeared with fresh garlic first (optional). Ladle in the soup on top of the bread, making sure each serving has pieces of the smooth hound, the fish with bones in, and a mantis shrimp.

ZERRI SOTTO PESTO

Fried and Marinated Picarel

from the Central Food Market in Livorno

Picarel are a simple fish beloved by the Livornese. Given their silvery grey color and orange-yellow stripes, you wouldn't think they'd be so inexpensive.
In Livorno, the favorite way of eating this fish is *sotto il pesto*, which in this case does not mean the pesto that probably comes to mind. Rather than the typical Ligurian pesto of basil, pine nuts and cheese, this is a pesto made of garlic and chili pepper—flavors strong enough to raise the dead! First the picarel are fried. Then the crunchy fish are marinated in a mixture of olive oil, vinegar, garlic and chili pepper.
A bit of patience is required, as they need to marinate for at least a day. When ready, they can be served as an appetite-stirring starter with a slice of fresh bread, or as a main dish with a boiled potato salad seasoned with garlic and parsley.

INGREDIENTS FOR 4 PEOPLE

500 g (just over 1 lb) picarel fish (or fresh anchovies)
500 ml (2 & ⅓ cups) quality seed oil
½ cup extra virgin olive oil
2 garlic cloves
1 dried chili pepper
½ cup red wine vinegar
salt

Clean the picarel by removing the guts and rinsing well with water. Dry the fish.

Fry the fish in plenty of quality seed oil for about 5 minutes, turning them from time to time, until they are golden and crunchy.

Traditional Livornese people will fry the fish whole with the bones, head and tail left intact. If you prefer a more refined style for this dish, you can clean them as you would anchovies, boned and opened flat.

Arrange the just-fried picarel on a plate covered with paper towels so the excess oil is absorbed.

Prepare the marinade. Add the olive oil to a small saucepan. Finely chop the garlic and crumble the chili. Add both to the pan. Heat until the garlic starts to brown. Add the vinegar and cook on the lowest heat for a few minutes.

Transfer the fish to a bowl, preferably a shallow terracotta bowl or similar. Lightly salt and cover with the marinade. Let rest for at least a day before eating so the flavors are well absorbed.

Covered in oil, the picarel can keep for a few days in the refrigerator.

TRIGLIE ALLA LIVORNESE

Livorno Style Mullet

from the Central Food Market in Livorno

This is a traditional Jewish dish. Livorno was once a carriage-free port town which welcomed Jews as it did people of every nationality and background. The freedoms guaranteed by the Livorno Constitution to whomever came to this city eätended to the Jews as well. Here they were not confined to ghettos, nor subjected to other limitations or humiliations. Expelled by Christian Spain, they arrived carrying a few tomato plants in Livorno, where they taught the local population—and then the rest of the country—how to cook with tomato. Thus many traditional Livornese dishes are rich with red tomato, dishes ranging from *cacciucco* fish soup to pan-cooked mullet. The mullets used here are red mullets, those with the shimmery, reddish-purple color—a color called *amaranto* in Italian. Interestingly, Amaranto is also the name of the Livorno soccer team, as celebrated in the 1930s as the red mullet of Livorno. Smaller mullets, those weighing less than 100 g, are very good for frying. They often end up in the typical mix of fish used in a fish fry. Those weighing 100 g can also be cooked in tomato sauce—the Livornese tomato sauce, to be precise. Those weighing 200 or 300 g are good for cooking *en papillote*, while those even larger can be grilled. Technically speaking, the recipe here for Livornese style red mullet is an economical one, yet its sauce is one of the most flavorful you can imagine.
One whiff of its aroma will have your mouth watering. Don't overlook the bread, a fundamental accompaniment to this dish.

INGREDIENTS FOR 4 PEOPLE

8 red mullets,
each weighing about 100 g (3 & ½ oz)
extra virgin olive oil
1 small bunch fresh parsley + more for garnishing
2 garlic cloves
500 g (just over 1 lb) peeled tomatoes
salt
red chili pepper (to taste)
fresh bread

Start by rinsing the fish well, then scaling and gutting it. Set the fish aside once it is rinsed and dried.

Finely chop the 2 garlic cloves together with the parsley. Cover the bottom of a large pan with oil and add the mince. Cook until the garlic begins to sizzle.

Purée the peeled tomatoes and add to the pan as soon as the garlic begins to brown. Adjust for salt and chili pepper and cook for about 10 minutes on low heat to create a thick, flavorful sauce (the best part of this dish).

Add the fish to the pan, carefully arranging them side by side.

Cook on low for about 10 minutes, without turning them. Red mullet is a delicate fish that shouldn't be touched while cooking. Simply cover them from time to time with the sauce.

Finish with a dusting of the fresh parsley and serve with plenty of fresh bread, as half the pleasure of this dish is dipping a chunk of bread into the wonderful sauce.

PESCE ALL'ISOLANA

Island Style Fish

from the Market of Orbetello by the Sea

Saturday morning before heading to the beach, stroll through the Orbetello market along the quay to enjoy the views of the lagoon. I can easily lose myself here in the sea aromas in the air that blend with the smells of fresh fish from the Fratelli Canuzzi stand. In moments like these, I find it's always best to put on your most sincere smile and ask for assistance.

"Could you recommend a local traditional recipe? Something simple and fish based, full of the colors and aromas of summer?"

"That's easy," was the response. "Pesce all'Isolana."

This very Mediterranean dish, whose name translates to something like "island style," is prepared over a bed of potatoes and cherry tomatoes, with a splash of white wine, and fish such as snapper, sea bream or sea bass. It is then covered with quality summer vegetables like zucchini, eggplants or carrots and cooked *en papillote*. With one dish you have a main course and a side, full of the flavors of summer.

INGREDIENTS FOR 2 PEOPLE

500 g (just over 1 lb) white fish (bream, snapper, bass), scaled and cleaned for oven cooking
extra virgin olive oil
350 g (¾ lb) potatoes
1 handful datterini tomatoes (or similar)
½ red onion
salt
black pepper
1 eggplant
2 light colored zucchini
½ cup white wine

Finely slice the potato and layer them in the bottom of a baking dish greased with extra virgin olive oil.

Cut the tomatoes in half and thinly slice the onion. Distribute both on top of the potatoes. Drizzle oil on top of all the vegetables, together with a dusting of salt and freshly ground black pepper.

Arrange the clean fish on top of the bed of vegetables and season with more olive oil, salt and pepper.

Finely slice the eggplant and zucchini to equal width so they cook uniformly, and cover the fish completely.

Season one last time with oil, salt and pepper. Add the white wine to keep the dish moist while cooking.

Cook at 180°C/350°F for 50 minutes, or until the fish begins to emit a lovely aroma. This is the sign it is ready.

Serve the fish sliced into fillets, accompanied by the vegetables.

SIDE DISHES

PISELLI ALLA FIORENTINA

Florentine Style Peas

from Sant'Ambrogio Market in Florence

Guido Peyron writes of this dish in his book *Note sulla Cucina e Altre Cose* (Notes on Cooking and Other Things), along with Paolo Petroni in his *The Complete Book of Florentine Cooking*. These peas are a side dish, one highly associated with Florence and its love for well-cooked vegetables, to be served in the sauce Wthat forms when stewed on low heat. It's a common side dish at Easter, served alongside roasted lamb.
Try any leftovers with a plate of pasta: lightly mash them (for better cling) and toss with pasta and a bit of fresh parsley. They're also very good as a spaghetti sauce. I shelled peas for the first time when I was already grown, at around age 28. Before then, peas for me were always frozen and out of a bag, good enough, but above all fast to prepare. Once you've tried freshly shelled peas, however, you realize how different the frozen ones are from the fresh, with the little thud they make as they land in the salad bowl, and their green springtime scent and delicate flavor.
You can spot them at the market from afar, these first signs of spring's arrival. At that moment, you realize that sunny days are soon to follow, along with lighter dishes, fresh-cut flowers in vases, and country walks.

INGREDIENTS FOR 4 PEOPLE

400 g (14 oz) shelled peas (about 1 kg or 2 lb with shells)
2 garlic cloves
1 small bunch fresh parsley
1 tsp sugar
salt
freshly ground black pepper
1 cup water
50 g (2 oz) pancetta, sliced into thin strips

Shell the peas and collect them in a bowl. As this recipe doesn't call for a sautéed mince to start, simply place the peas in a pot together with the garlic, parsley, sugar, salt and pepper.

Cover the mixture with a cup of water and let stew on low heat for about 40 to 45 minutes.

When the peas are nearly done, add the sliced pancetta and let cook together for a few minutes to flavor.

Let the peas rest for about 10 minutes before serving as a side dish, or as a main dish served with fresh bread to sop up their juices.

CROCCHETTE DI PATATE

Potato Croquettes

from Certaldo's Market

INGREDIENTS FOR 4 PEOPLE

FOR THE CROQUETTES

4 medium potatoes, boiled
4 tbsp aged Tuscan pecorino, grated
1 egg
salt
freshly ground black pepper
sunflower oil for frying

FOR THE BREADCRUMB COATING

1 egg, beaten
breadcrumbs

Smash the boiled potatoes. Add the egg and cheese and combine well. Adjust for salt and pepper. Make the croquettes using a spoon, shaping them into a cylindrical form.

Dip each croquette in the beaten egg and then into the breadcrumbs. Repeat until the croquettes are all covered.

Fry in plenty of boiling oil until golden. Serve immediately.

FAGIOLINI SERPENTI IN UMIDO

Stewed Snake Beans

from Piazza della Sala Market in Pistoia

Tuscan summers are all about refreshing recipes whose ingredients are meant to alleviate the intense heat—recipes like panzanella with cucumber and an invigorating dash of vinegar, or beans served cold with freshly ground black pepper, fresh onion, oil and vinegar. Interestingly, these are summer versions of various soups that provide warmth and comfort in winter.

On July 25, the people of Pistoia celebrate their patron, Saint James the Greater. The traditional lunch for this feast day, though far from refreshing, is deeply representative of local history and habits. At the center of the tradition is a Muscovy duck stewed in ample amounts of sauce so there's plenty for the *maccheroni* (very thin fresh egg pasta cut into squares). The meal's designated side dish are these stewed snake beans, often cooked directly in the tomato sauce in which the duck has been cooked.

Also known as asparagus beans or yardlong beans in English, these long, thin beans started appearing on the outskirts of Pistoia only recently, then began showing up at market stands throughout Tuscany. The recipe is not unlike several others my grandmother used to make when I was little, since stewed green beans are the summer side dish *par excellence*. Their nice flavor owes to a mince of seasonings and crumbled pancetta or prosciutto crudo. Served with fresh bread to dip in the savory juices, they often turn into my main course. They can be eaten much like spaghetti, twirled with a fork and lifted. Be sure to have plenty of napkins on hand, as the tomato sauce can be rather unforgiving!

INGREDIENTS FOR 4 PEOPLE

350 g (¾ lb) snake beans
1 garlic clove
1 small red onion
½ celery stalk
1 carrot
4 tbsp extra virgin olive oil
200 g (7 oz) ripe tomatoes
1 cup cold water
salt

Clean the beans by snapping off the end and pulling away the string that runs along the length of the bean.

Make a very fine mince of garlic, onion, celery and carrot. Add the oil to a very large pot (the beans take up a good deal of space).

Add the mince to the cold pot along with the beans.
Chop the tomato and add to the pot, followed by a cup of cold water.
Lightly salt (you can adjust for salt again at the end of cooking).

Cover the pot and cook for about 1 hour on low heat, checking often and mixing from time to time to prevent the beans from sticking.
Add small amounts of lukewarm water if they dry out too much.

The beans are ready when they are soft, have turned a dark green color and are covered in a coarse sauce (given the mince). Adjust for salt as needed and serve warm.

CARPACCIO DI OVOLI

Caesar's Mushroom Carpaccio

from Marradi's Market

When the first summer rains came, Grandma became restless. They would mark the beginning of the mushroom season, and she couldn't wait to venture into the woods, intrigued by the stories of those who had already found mushrooms. When Grazia and Maura, friends of grandma's, became part of our family, the mushroom hunting adventure became a regular autumn fixture, something to be enjoyed together. Grandma, Grazia, and Maura were famous for setting off and venturing into the thick of the woods, getting lost sometimes, always returning home by a different route, but invariably with something in the basket.
Dad also has an extraordinary eye for mushrooms: he rarely goes hunting for them but when he ventures into the woods he always comes home with a good haul. Porcini, *lardaioli*, but above all, *ovoli*. Grandma values the *ovoli*, also known as Caesar's mushrooms, even more than porcini. They are perfect when served raw, thinly sliced, simply dressed with extra virgin olive oil and lemon juice.

INGREDIENTS FOR 4 PEOPLE

- 450 g (1 lb) fresh Caesar's mushrooms
- juice of ½ lemon
- 4 tbsp of extra virgin olive oil
- fine sea salt
- freshly ground black pepper

Carefully clean the *ovoli*: use a damp paper towel or a soft mushroom brush to wipe each mushroom to remove any dirt. Slice them thinly, then arrange them on a plate.

Prepare an emulsion by beating together the lemon juice with the olive oil and a generous pinch of salt.

Drizzle the dressing over the sliced *ovoli*, add a few turns of black pepper, and serve the mushroom carpaccio as an appetizer.

INSALATA CON MIELE DI SPIAGGIA, NOCI E PARMIGIANO

Walnut, Parmigiano and Honey Salad

from the Farmers Market at the Ancient Forum Boarium in Lucca

This salad is based on all those foraged herbs that grow wild in the fields and along the hedgerows, herbs that I wish I had the skills to recognize, just like grandma does. Luckily there are stalls at the market that sell them, a riot of different colors, textures and shapes that turn a simple salad into an exciting journey.
A drizzle of a unique honey takes this salad to another level: it's *miele di spiaggia*, beach honey, produced by the Calafata farm: their beehives are set up on the dunes of the Migliarino San Rossore Park, a few hundred meters from the shoreline.
The bees are free to fly over the flowers of the pine forest and the beach, over the cistus, the strawberry tree, the tamarisk and, in particular, over the helichrysum, which grows on these beaches and gives the honey its unmistakable scent.

INGREDIENTS FOR 4 PEOPLE

300 g (10 oz) mixed salad leaves (endive, dandelion, wild arugula...)
85 g (3 oz) shelled walnuts, roughly chopped
55 g (2 oz) Parmigiano Reggiano, shaved
4 tbsp extra virgin olive oil
1 tbsp apple cider vinegar
fine sea salt
beach honey*

*You can replace the beach honey with chestnut honey, strawberry tree honey or a very aromatic millefiori.

Wash the salad well, dry it and collect it in a large bowl. Scatter the salad with the roughly chopped walnuts, then dress it with oil and vinegar and a pinch of salt. Toss the salad well to distribute the dressing evenly.

Let it sit for at least 15 minutes to soften the tough leaves, then add the shaved Parmigiano Reggiano and drizzle with honey. Serve it as an appetizer but also as a side dish to grilled meat.

CAVOLO STRASCICATO

Savoy Cabbage and Sausage

from Piazza Cavallotti's Market in Livorno

Antonio says, "Use one sausage per person". "This could be a hearty side dish, but also a main course to eat with plenty of bread for cleaning your plate."
This is how Antonio, known at the Piazza Cavallotti market as the "king of lettuce," explained the following recipe to me, with its fragrant garlic in a bit of olive oil, and chili pepper, too, that ingredient we now know to be vital and abundant in the Livornese cuisine.
The sausages here are not intended to merely add flavor or accompany bread, but rather play a more important role. The tomato and chili lend color and a touch of sweetness.
The cabbage is cut into thin strips and cooked very slowly over low heat, absorbing all the flavors that will delight your taste buds. Serve with fresh, crusty bread.

INGREDIENTS FOR 4 PEOPLE

2 garlic cloves
extra virgin olive oil
1 chili pepper
4 sausages
1 medium Savoy cabbage
2 San Marzano tomatoes (or similar)
salt

Finely chop 1 garlic clove and break the pepper into pieces.
Brown together in a few tablespoons of extra virgin olive oil.
Remove the sausage casings. Break up the sausage and cook in a pan for a few minutes.

Thinly slice the cabbage and add it to the pan, stirring to combine well with the sausage. Cube the tomatoes and add to the cabbage.
Stir and cover.

Cook for about 45 minutes on low heat, stirring occasionally. Should the dish dry out too much, add a few spoonfuls of warm water. Adjust for salt towards the end of the cooking time when the cabbage is very soft, and serve.

DESSERTS

TORTA DI SEMOLINO E CIOCCOLATO CON PERE

Semolina and Chocolate Cake with Pears

from Sant'Ambrogio Market in Florence

Browsing the stalls at Sant'Ambrogio's market, just before the colors of the fruit begin to change to orange with the arrival of all the citrus fruits, crates of apples and pears fill the air with their fall aromas. Usually the first dessert to come to mind here is apple cake, the classic version known since childhood. Not long ago I began to reconsider the pear, however, with its grainy and metallic taste and unique texture when cooked. I'll often pair them with cinnamon, fresh ginger, wine or, better still, chocolate.

INGREDIENTS FOR 8 PEOPLE

FOR THE PASTRY

150 g (⅔ cup) butter, room temperature
150 g (¾ cup) sugar
1 egg
300 g (2 & ⅓ cups) all-purpose
1 pinch of salt
zest of 1 lemon (organic, not chemically treated)

FOR THE SEMOLINA AND PEAR CREAM

500 ml (2 cups) whole milk
125 g (¾ cup) semolina flour
2 eggs
6 tbsp sugar
5 tbsp vinsanto
2 ripe pears, peeled and cubed

FOR THE CHOCOLATE GANACHE

250 ml (1 cup) whipping cream
250 g (9 oz) dark chocolate, cut into small pieces

Combine the butter and sugar until smooth, making sure no chunks of butter remain.

Add the egg and beat. Sift in the flour and salt and combine, followed by the lemon zest.

Work the dough quickly as to not let the butter warm, lightly press it down and cover with plastic wrap. Keep in the refrigerator for a few hours or overnight.

Next make the semolina cream. Warm the milk and sprinkle in the semolina, making sure no lumps form. Whisk continuously. When the milk reaches a boil or when the cream becomes firm, remove from heat and let cool, stirring periodically. When the cream is warm, add the eggs, sugar, and vinsanto. Lastly, add the pears.

Remove the pastry dough from the fridge. Roll out the dough to cover the bottom and sides of a baking dish 28 cm (about 11 inches) in diameter. Pour in the cream.

Bake at 180°C/350°F for 40 minutes or until the semolina cream just starts to turn golden.

Let the cake cook and prepare the ganache. Bring the cream to a boil and add the chocolate and stir to dissolve well. Slowly pour over the cake. Let the cake cool completely and place in the refrigerator for a few hours before serving. Remove from the fridge a half hour before serving and let cool to room temperature.

SETTEMBRE. LA SCHIACCIATA CON L'UVA

September: Schiacciata with Harvest Grapes

I remember well the flavor of just picked grapes. I was 19 years old and just about to head off to university. Towards the end of that summer, I decided to join in the grape harvest, a job that where I come from all young people eventually find themselves doing at some point, whether out of necessity, to pay for their vacations or just to earn a little something extra for the winter months.

The work started early in the morning, when the vine wires were still wet with dew, and continued on through the hottest time of day to finish around five in the afternoon. At first you could resist the grapes. Eventually though, almost without thinking, you'd end up popping one into your mouth, after which it was difficult to stop. That grape embodied so much: sour, sweet, refreshing, intoxicating. All the aroma and color and sweetness of that single just-picked grape are found in this grape *schiacciata*, my childhood snack whose flavor always signified the end of summer and the return to school.

Lacking nearby vineyards, head to the markets from mid-August to the end of September to find clusters of wine grapes, the best kind for making this *schiacciata*. You'll have to get there early. Many a market-goer remembers the flavor of *schiacciata all'uva* as I do, and with just a small basket of grapes available most days, they will be gone within a few hours.

The method here is almost exactly that of the olive oil *schiacciata*: start the day prior, let the poolish ripen, then the first kneading. The next day make the *schiacciata*. In the past this *schiacciata* was simply a portion of bread dough from the week's baking, to which sugar and grapes would be added. It was then baked in the baker's large wood-fired ovens to test the heat inside.

SCHIACCIATA CON L'UVA

Schiacciata with Harvest Grapes

from Colle Val d'Elsa Market

INGREDIENTS FOR 2 BAKING PANS MEASURING 33 X 25 CM (13 X 10 INCHES)

FOR THE POOLISH

1 g (about 1⁄16 of a 0.6-oz cake) fresh yeast
250 g (1 & ¾ cups) bread flour
250 g (1 cup) cold water

FOR THE DOUGH

poolish made prior
500 g (4 cups) all-purpose flour
5 g (¾ tsp) salt
2 tbsp extra virgin olive oil, plus more for greasing the pans
1 tsp acacia flower honey
250 g (1 cup) slightly lukewarm water
300 g (⅔ lb) wine grapes
200 g (1 cup) sugar

Make the poolish the day before: I suggest making it around dinner time, as it requires at least 12 hours of ripening. Dissolve the yeast in cold water in a large bowl, then add the strong flour and whisk to remove any clumps. Cover the bowl with plastic wrap and let rest at room temperature until the next day. The poolish is ready after 12 hours.

To make the dough, place the poolish in a large bowl. Add the flour, salt, honey and olive oil. Begin to knead the dough, adding the water slowly so it is absorbed. Knead for at least 10 minutes, at the end of which the dough should be firm and not too sticky.

Lightly oil your hands and form a ball with the dough.
Oil the bowl and place the dough inside. Cover with plastic wrap and let ripen at room temperature until the dough has doubled in size, at least 3 hours.

When the dough has risen, oil your hands again and gently deflate it. Divide into 4 equal parts.

Oil the two baking pans. Roll out two portions of the dough directly in each pan, letting it relax after each time you press it outwards.

Meanwhile, roll out the other two portions of dough on a well-floured pastry board. Use your hands and again try to spread out the dough gradually.

Cover the dough in the pans with half of the sugar and then sprinkle most of the grapes on top. Cover each with one of the remaining rolled out dough sheets, and seal the borders well.

Let rise at room temperature for at least 2 hours, then cover the top with the remaining sugar and a drizzle of olive oil.
Press the remaining grapes into the top layer of dough.
Heat the oven to 190°C/375°F. Bake for at least 20 to 25 minutes, until the *schiacciata* is puffed and golden.

LATTE ALLA PORTOGHESE ALLO ZAFFERANO

Crème Caramel with Saffron

from Greve in Chianti Market

When I was little, this was always the dessert served to celebrate important occasions. There's a family story behind it, too. About 40 years ago, my grandmother, my aunt Antonietta and her cousin Vivetta decided to meet for lunch, eager for company and the joys of a nice chat. Being modern women and rather ahead of their time, they each brought something along to the lunch. Aunt Antonietta took care of dessert that day, delighting her companions with her *latte alla portoghese*, a flan-like custard whose name derives from the Italian habit of referring to crème caramel as "Portuguese milk." It was how my grandmother learned about this recipe, a simple dessert calling for very few ingredients.

INGREDIENTS FOR 8 PEOPLE
YOU WILL NEED 8 INDIVIDUAL PORTION RAMEKINS, OR 2 MOLDS OF 26 CM IN LENGTH (ABOUT 10 INCHES)

1 g (0.035 oz) saffron pistils
1 l (4 & 1/4 cups) whole milk
zest of 1 lemon (organic, not chemically treated)
8 eggs
6 tbsp sugar
200 g (1 cup) sugar for the caramel

Start by toasting the saffron to enhance its flavor and fragrance (and reduce the amount needed as a result). Warm a heavy pot with a small amount of water until the base is well warmed. Place the saffron between two sheets of baking paper and set this on top of the hot pot. Let toast for 30 minutes.

When ready, crumble the saffron inside the baking paper. There's no need to make a fine powder, as some chunks of saffron pistils are a nice esthetic touch.

Heat the milk with the lemon zest until it boils, then remove from the heat and add the crumbled saffron. Mix well to dissolve and set aside for at least 20 minutes.

Beat the egg with the sugar until it is completely blended, but do not mix more than necessary or it will become too fluffy. Combine the milk with the egg, mixing until a liquid and consistent cream forms.

To make the caramel, pour the sugar into a non-stick pan and melt on medium heat, without mixing but rather tilting the pan, until a golden caramel forms.

Cover the bottoms of the ramekins with the caramel, then pour in the milk and egg mixture. Carefully arrange the ramekins inside a large baking dish filled with a couple inches of water. Bake at 160°C/320°F for 45 to 50 minutes, or until the cream is firm.

Remove from the oven and let cool. Place in the fridge for a few hours. To serve, turn out each portion onto a serving plate so that the caramel is on top of the crème.

PANFORTE

Sienese Fruit and Nut Cake

from the Christmas Market in Siena

The origins of *panforte* begin in the medieval monasteries of the area, where this "strong bread" would be prepared for special occasions. Later *panforte* passed to the hands of local apothecaries, those with access to rare and precious ingredients like sugar, almonds, candied fruit and spices.
Spice is what makes *panforte* special, in fact. Its intense, honeyed aroma is for me the true smell of Christmas, as are the almonds and orange zest of *ricciarelli* cookies.
Recipes for *panforte* abound, some more traditional than others, such as the version Righi Parenti make.
This is my version, which I settled on after years of experimenting in the kitchen to perfect the balance of honey, almonds, candied fruit, sugar and spices.

INGREDIENTS FOR A PANFORTE 18 CM IN DIAMETER (ABOUT 7 INCHES)

300 g (10 & ½ oz) almonds, unpeeled
150 g (5 oz) candied orange zest
150 g (5 oz) candied citron zest
150 g (1 & ¼ cups) all-purpose flour
10 g (5 & ¼ tsp) spices for panforte *
200 g (⅔ cup) wildflower honey
1 sheet wafer paper
150 g (1 & ¼ cups) powdered sugar, plus more for dusting

* Every spice seller has his own ideas about quantities. I follow those used by Giovanni Righi Parenti: 5 g coriander powder, 3 g ground macis, 1 g ground clove, 1 g ground nutmeg.

Melt the honey, powdered sugar and 3 tbsp of water in a small saucepan over low heat. Remove the pan from the heat when the honey and sugar are completely melted to a golden syrup.

Combine the other ingredients in a bowl, then pour in the syrup and mix well with a spoon. You should have a dense batter.

Pour the batter into the springform pan lined with the wafer paper. Even out the surface using a wet spoon.

Dust the surface with powdered sugar and bake for 25 to 30 minutes at 180°C/355°F. Remove from the oven and let cool slightly before releasing the pan's spring. Do not wait too long otherwise the sugar will harden and make this step difficult.

Once cooled, dust generously with powdered sugar. Store for weeks wrapped in baking paper.

GATTÒ

Gâteau

from Arezzo's Market

This is one of Arezzo's most beloved desserts, known throughout Tuscany by different names, such as *salame dolce* ("sweet" salami), *tronco* (trunk), *rotolo* (roll) or the charming name we use in my house, *rotolino* (little roll). In Arezzo though it's called *gattò*, most likely influenced by the French *gâteau*. My grandmother would make this for my sister Claudia when she was little, as she was a very thin child and not really as interested in food as I was. The method can seem challenging, yet once you get the hang of it, it will come off without a hitch. Before you know it, you'll be masterfully making your own rolled up sponge cake, filled with your choice of cream, chocolate, jam or coffee ricotta mousse. Follow your instincts and you're sure to be pleased with the results. If you cannot find Alchermes—an Italian liqueur made by infusing cinnamon, clove, nutmeg and various other spices, whose uniquely red color derives from the traditional use of cochineal, or Kermes, insects—substitute with another spiced liqueur or coffee.

INGREDIENTS FOR 8 PEOPLE

FOR THE SPONGE ROLL CAKE
150 g egg whites (from about 5 eggs)
125 g (⅔ cup) caster sugar
100 g egg yolk (about 6)
100 g (¾ cup) all-purpose flour
50 g (¼ cup) cornstarch
butter to grease the baking paper

FOR THE ALCHERMES SYRUP
100 ml (½ cup) water
50 g (¼ cup) sugar
50 ml (¼ cup) Alchermes

FOR THE FILLING
500 ml (2 cups) whole milk
seeds of 1 vanilla pod
2 eggs
4 tbsp sugar
2 tbsp potato starch
200 g (7 oz) small pieces of dark chocolate

TO SERVE
powdered sugar for dusting

Make the Alchermes syrup. Boil the water and sugar until the sugar is completely dissolved. Add the Alchermes and let cool before using.

Next make the vanilla cream and the chocolate cream.

Start by bringing the milk to a boil with the vanilla seeds. Set aside.

Whisk the eggs and sugar with the cornstarch, then pour the milk in slowly, mixing continuously to prevent the eggs from cooking. Transfer the cream to a small saucepan and heat on low, whisking continuously until the cream begins to thicken.

Remove the cream from the heat and divide into two equal portions. To one of the portions, add the broken chocolate pieces and stir until the chocolate is completely melted. Let both creams cool.

Now make the sponge roll cake. Heat the oven to 250°C/475°F.

Beat the egg whites with 75 grams (6 tablespoons) of sugar until stiff. Beat the yolks separately with the remaining sugar until they are light and frothy. Gently combine the two.

Sift the flour with the potato starch and fold into the cream, using gentle upward movements (from the bottom towards the top).

CONTINUED ON PAGE 324

CONTINUATION OF PAGE 323

Line a large baking dish with baking paper and then grease the paper with butter. This will allow the cake to come away easier.

Pour the batter into the dish, maintaining a uniform thickness of maximum 1 cm (about ½ inch). Cook for about 5 minutes, until it starts to color.

Meanwhile, dampen a tea towel and spread it out on a table.
As soon as the sponge cake is done, remove from the oven and transfer it onto the towel. Carefully detach it from the baking paper and roll it up, being careful not to break it.
Let it rest for a few minutes.
Unroll it and brush on the Alchermes syrup.

Spread the chocolate cream and the white cream in alternating stripes onto the sponge roll cake, and then rolling up the cake again, very carefully.

Wrap the gattò tightly with plastic wrap and refrigerate for a few hours.
Before serving, remove the plastic wrap and dust with powdered sugar.
Slice and serve.

La Bottega di

TIRAMISÙ

Five Rules for a Perfect Homemade Tiramisù

1 Don't skimp on quality. This may seem obvious enough, but the quality of ingredients makes all the difference. Choose a mascarpone that is not too liquid or lumpy, the very best ladyfinger cookies (called *savoiardi* in Italian) and an excellent dark chocolate. Although only a small amount is used of this last ingredient, those few shavings of crunchy chocolate layered in are the extra something special that significantly improves your tiramisù.

2 Beat and mix all the ingredients thoroughly, starting with the egg yolks and sugar until they turn white and frothy and the sugar is completely dissolved. To test the consistency, rub a small amount between your fingers: if you don't feel any grains of sugar then you can proceed. Then beat the egg whites until very stiff. There's nothing worse than that hint of liquid at the bottom of a bowl of egg whites that have not been adequately whipped, as this will compromise the consistency of the mascarpone cream, which holds the entire tiramisù together.

3 Whether you use classic coffee or instead opt for tea, make sure they are not sweetened. When called for, it's these well-balanced contrasts in flavor that render dishes interesting. And in this case, the bitter coffee flavor helps to temper the sweetness of the mascarpone cream.

4 Dip the cookies into the coffee (or tea) quickly, and just long enough to coat the two sides. If you leave the cookies too long in the liquid, the tiramisù will turn out too liquid and the cookies will be too weak to support the layers.

5 Tiramisù can be served traditionally, cut into square portions from a baking dish, or in individual serving dishes. In either case, place it in the fridge for a few hours prior to serving. Enjoy your tiramisù after letting it chill for a short while to allow the flavors to come together.

CHINA
ANTICA OFFICINA FARMACEUTICA DOTT. CLEMENTI
CHINA

CHINA

TIRAMISÙ CON LA CHINA

Tiramisù with China

from Fivizzano's Market

Just down the road from Piazza Medicea is Farmacia Clementi, an old-fashioned pharmacy providing standard services while simultaneously reflecting a true piece of Fivizzano history. Some old-time touches include splendid wooden window displays of medicinal herbs, spices, extracts, tablets and curative mixtures. The most precious product available here, however, is the famous China Clementi, a tonic and digestive elixir created in 1884 as an antimalarial medicine, made from two prized varieties of tropical China (*Cinchona Calisaya* and the rare Succirubra) along with other aromatic and medicinal herbs.
The Italian journalist Indro Montanelli, who was very fond of China Clementi, wrote that for him it was like "a delightful memory, a return to the good, real things of my childhood."
Today it is still made according to the same craft method and 19th-century recipe, sought by famous bartenders the world over for special cocktails. I mix it with coffee and include it in my favorite dessert, tiramisù. If you cannot find China, substitue with the walnut liqueur *nocino* or a coffee liqueur.

INGREDIENTS FOR 8 PEOPLE

250 ml (1 & ⅛ cup) whole milk
2 large egg yolks
60 grams (⅓ cup) granulated sugar
15 grams (2 tablespoons) cornstarch
250 g (9 oz) mascarpone
200 ml (¾ cup) brewed coffee
6 tbsp China or other liqueur
100 g (3 & ½ oz) ladyfinger cookies
50 g (1 & ¾ oz) dark chocolate
unsweetened cocoa powder

Heat the milk over medium flame and remove it as soon as it steams.

In a large saucepan, whisk the egg yolks with sugar and cornstarch until smooth. Slowly pour the hot milk in a thin stream into the egg mixture, whisking constantly.

Move the saucepan over medium-low heat and cook, whisking constantly. As soon as the mixture starts to thicken, remove it from the heat.

Add the mascarpone and 2 tbsp of China (or other liqueur), and mix it in with a whisk or electric beaters until smooth. Refrigerate until cold.

Finely chop the dark chocolate.

Combine the coffee and 4 tbsp of China in a bowl.

Prepare the tiramisù by alternating layers of the ladyfingers (dipped in the liquid), the mascarpone cream and the chopped chocolate.

Finish with a top layer of the mascarpone cream and a dusting of unsweetened cocoa powder. Let the tiramisù rest in the fridge for a few hours before serving.

TORTA SQUISITA

"Exquisite" Cake

from Castelnuovo di Garfagnana's Market

What can we expect from a cake with such a name if not something utterly exquisite? Ricotta tarts are one of the most popular desserts in Garfagnana, and rather beloved throughout all of Italy. This local version calls for candied fruits and dark chocolate. Use plenty of chocolate, even if it seems out of proportion with the other ingredients, and chop it roughly so some bites of the tart include large pieces.

INGREDIENTS FOR 8 PEOPLE

FOR THE PASTRY

- 150 g (⅔ cup) butter, room temperature
- 150 g (¾ cup) sugar
- 1 egg, beaten
- 300 g (2 & ⅓ cups) all-purpose flour
- zest of 1 lemon
- 1 pinch of salt

FOR THE FILLING

- 400 g (1 & ⅔ cups) ricotta
- 100 g (½ cup) sugar
- 3 eggs
- 150 g (5 oz) dark chocolate
- 100 g (3 & ½ oz) candied orange and citron zest
- ¼ cup Sassolino liqueur (or Strega or *vinsanto*)

Mix the butter and sugar until well combined and no large pieces of butter remain.

Add the egg. Incorporate the flour, lemon zest and a pinch of salt.

Work the dough quickly as to not let the butter warm, bringing the ingredients together, then lightly press the dough down and cover with plastic wrap. Keep in the refrigerator for a few hours or overnight.

Make the filling. Sieve the ricotta and combine with the beaten egg and sugar. Cube the candied zests and roughly chop the chocolate. Add both to the mixture along with the Sassolino or other liqueur.

Heat the oven to 180°C/350°F.

Remove the pastry from the fridge and knead until adequately malleable. Using a rolling pin and flour, roll out the dough to a thickness of 5 mm (less than ¼ of an inch).

Butter and flour a round springform cake pan 22 cm in diameter (about 9 inches). Lay the dough in the pan and cut the excess from the edges.

Fill the tart with the ricotta cream. Decorate the top with leftover strips of pastry. Bake for about 40 minutes until the tart is golden. Let cool completely before slicing.

CASTAGNACCIO CON LE MELE

Apple Chestnut Cake

from Barga's Market

Castagnaccio is an ancient recipe, a dessert that speaks to the Tuscan peasant woman's triumph over poverty and hunger. The simplest version involves a basic mix of chestnut flour, water, oil and rosemary, resulting in a cake with an almost biting, smoky flavor and a texture similar to bread pudding. And yet *castagnaccio* is in some ways a surprisingly modern dessert. It contains no sugar, and is naturally gluten and lactose free. More elaborate versions call for dried fruit and raisins to be added along with its fundamental ingredient, of course: chestnut flour. Its name derives from *castagna*, the Italian word for chestnut. The first time you taste it, *castagnaccio*'s floury texture melts in your mouth along with its sweet chestnut flavor—a flavor that for we who grew up with it evokes memories of children in winter coats and woolen gloves, of a warm paper bag containing 1,000 lire's worth of roasted chestnuts, the shop lights seen from the street with mother and father, and the sweet taste of this timeless winter treat. When I tasted Alessandro Manfredini's version from Garfagnana I started adding orange zest and walnuts to my *castagnaccio*, while following my father in law's approach, I now like to top it with apples.

INGREDIENTS FOR A BAKING DISH 26 CM IN DIAMETER (ABOUT 10 INCHES)

50 g (1 & ¾ oz) raisins
1 tbsp vinsanto
250 g (2 cups) chestnut flour
1 pinch of salt
400 ml (1 & ⅔ cups) water
50 g (1 & ¾ oz) walnuts, roughly chopped
zest of ½ an orange
1 apple, cored and thinly sliced
2 tbsp sugar
1 sprig rosemary
extra virgin olive oil

Heat the oven to 180°C/350°F. In a small bowl, soak the raisins in a small amount of tepid water and 1 tbsp of vinsanto.

Sift the chestnut flour into a large bowl and add a pinch of salt. Pour in the water a little at a time, mixing continuously to prevent clumps. Add the grated orange zest. Drain the raisins, squeeze out the excess liquid and add them to the mixture along the walnuts. Combine thoroughly.

Grease a baking dish with plenty of extra virgin olive oil. Pour in the batter, then decorate the top with the apple slices. Sprinkle the sugar and rosemary needles on top of the apples. Drizzle with olive oil and bake for about 50 to 55 minutes, until the apples are caramelized. *Castagnaccio* can be eaten at room temperature or cold.

CREMA AL MASCARPONE CON CIALDE DI MONTECATINI

Mascarpone Cream with Montecatini Cookies

from Montecatini Earth Market

During the 1920s, in the midst of the Belle Époque, Montecatini was a famous thermal spa destination, frequented by members of high society and elite travellers. It was a lively town, rich with possibilities and luxury hotels. It was at this time a Jewish family of pastry makers from Czecho-Slovakia moved here and opened a business next to the Leopoldine Spa. Among their many popular creations was a thin and crunchy round wafer cookie, made with no fats but rather only egg, sugar and flour, and filled with a sugary almond paste. They were soon to win over Montecatini's tourists and residents alike with their creation. In the 1930s, with war in the air, the family decided to leave Montecatini in search of a safer home. They sold their business—along with the secret wafer recipe—to Orlando Bargilli, a former railway worker who took to his new profession with enthusiasm. Today the business still makes the wafers as it did in the past, cooked perfectly without butter and filled with sugar and almonds from Puglia. They go well with tea or coffee, as a breakfast cookie, or with vanilla ice cream or mascarpone cream and vinsanto.

INGREDIENTS FOR 8 PEOPLE

2 large egg yolks
60 grams (⅓ cup) granulated sugar
250 g (9 oz) mascarpone
1 small glass vinsanto
250 g (9 oz) fresh whipping cream
500 g (just over 1 lb) strawberries
4 Montecatini wafer cookies

Beat the egg yolks and the sugar with an electric beater until light and frothy. The cream is ready when you can no longer feel the grains of sugar between your fingers.

Add the mascarpone and vinsanto and briskly combine to obtain a smooth cream. In a separate bowl, lightly whip the cream until you just have soft peaks.

Gently fold the whipped cream into the mascarpone with a spatula, working from the bottom upwards. Refrigerate for a few hours.

Rinse the strawberries and cut the larger ones in half. Arrange the strawberries in small dessert cups and add a few spoonfuls of the cream. Garnish each cup with half a Montecatini wafer, broken into pieces.

BISCOTTI. QUATTRO RICETTE

Biscotti. Four Recipes

The word *biscotto* means "baked twice" in Italian, a perfectly apt description of how these cookies are made. Today, Prato almond cookies are called either *biscotti* or *cantucci*. Yet in the past these two types of cookies were rather different, despite their shared baking method. The idea of cooking baked goods twice was a response to an important demand, that of conserving bread and other products for long periods.
The earliest cookies date to the Roman era, prepared with barley, honey and wine. Later, *biscotti* transformed into different varieties, thanks to spices and dried fruit made available by commercial exchange with The East. And it was introduction of sugar in the 13th century that would ultimately launch a revolution in pastry making. During this time period, *cantucci* acquired their identity, as strips of bread spiced with anise and fennel seeds, cut lengthwise and baked a second time in the oven. This everyday cookie would be dunked in sweet wine, and was thought to possess invigorating qualities that would "sort out" the stomach.

The almond *biscotti* known as *bischotelli* are baked in the same manner, but with different ingredients. These were considered the so-called "sweet table" desserts, always on hand in homes of a certain status. And they were costlier and more refined, given the use of not only almonds but also egg, an ingredient that would have classified them immediately as a luxury item.

In 1858, Antonio Mattei opened his *biscotti* factory in Prato, at Via Ricasoli 11.
The Mattei bakery made great quantities of spiced *cantucci* and almond *biscotti*, which together with the significant national and international recognition they received earned the label "*biscotti of Prato.*" In 1908 the bakery passed to the Pandolfini family, who after three generations of business continue to produce wonderful biscotti that taste of home and tradition, following the original recipe developed by Antonio Mattei in 1858. It's not easy to pinpoint a specific recipe, as variations abound, each fiercely guarded by bakers, writers and families alike.

CANTUCCI

Almond Biscotti

from Prato's Market

After years of teaching cooking classes, I finally arrived at this version of *cantucci*. It's a recipe dear to me, one that represents the right balance between a hard cookie (good for dunking in vinsanto or coffee) and a cookie to enjoy on its own, whenever the mood strikes.

INGREDIENTS FOR 8 PEOPLE

FOR THE DOUGH

3 eggs
220 g (1 & ⅛ cups) sugar
280 g (2 & ¼ cups) all-purpose flour
5 g (1 full tsp) baking powder
zest of 1 organic orange
1 pinch of salt

FOR THE BASIC ALMOND RECIPE

200 g (7 oz) unskinned almonds

FOR THE DARK CHOCOLATE AND HAZELNUTS

150 g (5 oz) unskinned hazelnuts
100 g (3 & ½ oz) dark chocolate, chopped

FOR THE WHITE CHOCOLATE AND PISTACHIO VARIATION

120 g (4 & ¼ oz) unsalted pistachios
100 g (3 & ½ oz) white chocolate, chopped

FOR THE WHOLE WHEAT BISCOTTI WITH HONEY AND WALNUTS

1 pinch of salt
200 g (7 oz) walnuts
100 g (½ cup) cane sugar

BASIC RECIPE FOR ALMOND BISCOTTI (pictured overleaf)

Heat the oven to maximum, or 250°C/475°F. Put two eggs plus one yolk in a bowl. Keep the whites of the separated egg to use later. Beat the eggs with the sugar in a stand mixer or electric whisk until light and frothy. Sift in the flour together with the baking powder and salt. Add the orange zest. Add the almonds and combine thoroughly.

Cover a baking sheet with baking paper. Using a spatula, form two cylindrical shapes of the dough, each about 30 cm (12 inches) in length and no wider than 8 cm (a little over 3 inches). Beat the egg white with a fork until frothy and brush onto the dough shapes.

Lower the oven to 180°C/350°F and transfer the baking sheet to the oven. The very high temperature will prevent the dough from expanding too much during baking. Bake for about 20 minutes, until the shapes are golden on the outside but still moist inside. When pressed, the surface should be firm but give slightly.

Let cool for about 5 minutes. With a very sharp knife, slice the forms on a cutting board into cookie shapes about 2 cm thick (1 inch). Place the cookies back on the baking sheet and bake for another 15 to 18 minutes, until they are golden. Let cool completely on a rack. *Cantucci* will keep for weeks stored in a cookie jar or tin.

VARIATIONS

Slight adjustments to this basic *biscotti* recipe yield tasty results. Add hazelnut and dark chocolate or pistachios with white chocolate for a more elegant cookie, or try a whole wheat version with cane sugar, honey and walnuts. The method is the same as above. The endless possibilities make these *biscotti* the perfect Christmas gift. You can make them weeks in advance and store in a well-closed cookie tin.

BALLOTTE, BRUCIATE, UBRIACHE

Boiled, Roasted, or Wine-Soaked Chestnuts

Chestnuts have a true cult following in Mugello, given their fundamental role in times past as a means of sustenance, as well as the deep respect locals hold for the tree (sometimes called the "bread tree") and its fruit. Talk of chestnuts can also turn reductive rather quickly here, since in Marradi the *marron buono,* a slightly larger variety that has earned IGP status, tends to dominate. This versatile chestnut is perfect for making quality *marrons glacés.*

For years, chestnuts have been the backbone of food sustenance for local mountain populations. My grandmother once told me that when she was little, on her way to school she would pass by the mill where one of her classmates lived, and they both would fill their pockets with dried chestnuts to snack on that morning. The sweet nuts were a real treat for my grandma, who today still has rather a sweet tooth.

These days roasted chestnuts are found on every street corner in wintertime. A dozen or so wrapped in a paper cone is the best way to warm one's hands, too.

At home with friends, we often end our fall dinners with chestnuts, especially when the fire is blazing so we can roast them in the traditional manner, using an iron pan with holes.

CASTAGNE

Chestnuts

from Marradi's Market

INGREDIENTS FOR 4 PEOPLE

FOR THE BOILED CHESTNUTS

1 kg (just over 1 lb) *marroni* chestnuts (or other variety)
water
2 bay leaves
1 tbsp fennel seeds
1 tsp salt

FOR THE ROASTED CHESTNUTS

1 kg (just over 1 lb) *marroni* chestnuts (or other variety)

FOR THE ROASTED CHESTNUTS SOAKED IN WINE

1 kg (just over 1 lb) *marroni* chestnuts (or other variety)
sugar
red wine

BOILED CHESTNUT

Bring a pot of water to the boil. Add the bay leaves, fennel seeds and salt. Add the chestnuts and cook for 25 to 30 minutes.

Let the water cool. Start to peel the chestnuts by making an incision in each with a small sharp knife. Keep the chestnuts in the water as you peel them, which facilitates this long and painstaking task since the water softens the skins.

ROASTED CHESTNUTS

Make an incision in the skin of each chestnut on the lower part or the "belly." The best way to roast chestnuts to release all their sweet and toasted flavor is over an open fire, in an iron pan with holes made especially for this purpose. Lacking such a pan, you can use a cast iron or non-stick pan on your stove burners. Toss them often to roast evenly. They are ready when the skins are burnt and opened at the point of the incision. Transfer to a paper bag for about 10 minutes, then clean them by removing the burnt outer layer and the light-colored skin.

ROASTED CHESTNUTS SOAKED IN WINE

Start by roasting the chestnuts according to the instructions in the previous recipe. Peel the chestnuts and place in a large soup bowl or tureen. Dust them with a few tablespoons of sugar and cover in red wine. Let soak for at least 30 minutes before eating.

PERE VOLPINE AL VINO ROSSO

Volpina Pears in Red Wine

from Marradi's Market

How many types of pears do you know of? How many apple varieties can you recognize in the supermarket produce section? That is, aside from the usual four or five varieties with their respective shapes, colors and flavors. But beyond these widely known types, there's a fascinating world of variety—the so-called forgotten fruits.
Luckily they've not all been forgotten, at least not by farmers and small producers. It's still possible to find fruits with oddly sounding names at places like food festivals and market fairs, mostly pears and apples. Several local producers in Marradi, especially those from the Brisighella area in Romagna, bring crates of interesting apples to market: knobby apples and apples that seem frozen inside or taste of lemon line up alongside sorbs and jujubes. The very small, firm and sour pear variety known as Volpina is generally stored from autumn until Christmas time. They scent the house with their lovely fragrance, and are delicious cooked in red wine. The recipe from Romagna calls for sugar and Sangiovese wine, but I make these with Chianti. While spiced and sweetly intoxicating on their own, they also pair well with vanilla ice cream, rice pudding, panna cotta or chocolate cake.

INGREDIENTS FOR 4 PEOPLE

2 Volpina pears
(or other small, sour variety)
750 ml (3 cups) Chianti wine
2 tbsp brown sugar
1 stick cinnamon
2 star anise seeds

Peel the pears, leaving the stems in place. Line them up in a large saucepan or casserole dish and cover with the wine and brown sugar. Add the cinnamon stick and the star anise seeds. Cook on low heat for about an hour, covered.

Let cool and serve with the sauce formed during the cooking.
The pears can be served alone or accompanied by vanilla ice cream.

TORTA COI BISCHERI

Pisan Rice and Chocolate Pie with Candied Fruits

from the Farmers Market in Piazza Santa Caterina in Pisa

My family has always loved cakes made with rice, considered the ideal desserts for celebrating birthdays and special occasions. These simple, fast cakes manage to win over everyone with little effort, thanks to their moist, creamy filling of chocolate, candied fruits, raisins and pine nuts, and they pair nicely with a coffee or a glass of vinsanto at the close of a family meal. Among the many variations there's also rice and cream, ricotta and cream and chard and raisins. Its name will likely make a Tuscan smile, since *bischero*—which here refers to the strips of pastry on top—is a local slang word for a fool or idiot, someone easily taken in. *Bischero* is also a word for a tuning peg for violins and guitars, from which these decorative strips of pastry actually take their name.

INGREDIENTS FOR A BAKING DISH 20 CM IN DIAMETER (ABOUT 8 INCHES)

FOR THE PASTRY

250 g (2 cups) all-purpose flour
1 egg
100 g (½ cup) sugar
100 g (½ cup) butter, room temperature

FOR THE FILLING

100 g (½ cup) originario rice
1 pinch of salt
1 egg
100 g (½ cup) sugar
150 g dark chocolate
2 tbsp vinsanto
50 g (1 & ¾ oz) raisins, soaked and drained
50 g (1 & ¾ oz) pine nuts
50 g (1 & ¾ oz) candied citron, cut into thin strips
seeds of ½ a vanilla pod
1 pinch of cinnamon

Start by making the shortcrust pastry. Combine the butter with the sugar and egg. Add the flour and knead just enough to form a ball. Wrap the dough in plastic wrap and place in the fridge for a few hours.

To make the filling, start by cooking the rice in plenty of boiling water and a pinch of salt (follow the package instructions, but 12 minutes should suffice).

Drain the rice and transfer to a bowl. Add the grated chocolate, sugar, the beaten egg and vinsanto. Next add the raisins, the candied citron and the pine nuts. Lastly add the cinnamon and vanilla seeds.

Butter and flour a round springform cake pan 20 cm in diameter (about 8 inches).

Remove the pastry from the refrigerator. Roll it out to about 5 cm thick (2 inches), using a rolling pin and a small amount of flour. Cover the cake pan with the pastry, leaving at least 4 cm of border.

Add the filling. To decorate the borders, cut the extra pastry diagonally and fold the pieces onto themselves. Make the classic strips used to form a criss-cross pattern across the top.

Heat the oven to 180°C/350°F. Bake the cake for about 30 to 35 minutes, until the pastry is golden. Let cool completely before slicing.

FRATI

Livornese Donuts

from Piazza Cavallotti's Market in Livorno

The Antica Friggitoria is located in the heart of Livorno in Piazza Cavallotti (formerly Piazza delle Erbe), not far from the historic central food market. The specialty here are called *frati*, soft, sugar-coated donuts that vanish in a few bites, leaving behind sugar-covered lips and an immediate yearning for another. Take a close look at these pastries and you'll understand both how they earned their name and how much the Livornese love to joke: *frati* means friar, and these donuts bear a resemble to a monk's tonsure!

INGREDIENTS FOR ABOUT 26 DONUTS (AND 26 DONUTS HOLES)

FOR THE BIGA
1 g (1⁄16 a 0.6 oz cake) fresh yeast
100 g (½ cup) cold water
200 g (1 & ⅔ cups) bread flour

FOR THE DOUGH
biga made prior
10 g (⅔ of a 0.6 oz cake) fresh yeast
350 g (1 & ½ cups) tepid water
300 g (2 & ⅓ cups) bread flour
600 g (4 & ¾ cups) all-purpose flour
200 g (1 cup) sugar
+ more for dusting
zest of 1 orange
seeds of 1 vanilla pod
4 g (⅔ tsp) salt
150 g (⅔ cup) butter,
room temperature
500 ml (2 & ⅓ cups)
quality seed oil

Make the biga the evening prior. Dissolve the yeast in the water. Add the flour and stir just enough to combine, making sure there are no lumps. Cover the bowl with plastic wrap and let rest at room temperature for at least 12 hours.

Next make the dough. Dissolve the yeast in half of the tepid water in a stand mixer bowl. Add the biga, flours, sugar, vanilla seeds and grated orange zest. Begin to knead and slowly add in the remaining water.

Knead on low until a smooth, elastic, moist dough forms. Add the salt and the butter in pieces and continue kneading until the butter is completely incorporated. You should have a uniform, sticky dough.

Form a ball shape and place in a bowl greased with a small amount of oil. Cover with a damp tea towel. Let ripen in a warm, protected space, such as inside the oven with the light on. The dough should double in volume over 2 to 3 hours.

Remove the dough from the bowl. Using a small amount of flour, roll the dough to a thickness of about 1.5 cm (0.4 inches). Cut out the frati using a 15-cm (6 inches) round pastry cutter. Cut out a hole in each pastry using a smaller cutter and place each hole next to the donut.

Knead the leftover dough again and roll out another sheet to make the next batch of frati.

Cover everything with dry tea towel and let rest for 1 hour.

When the hour is up, fry the donuts in plenty of hot oil. Fry in batches, turning them every 20 to 30 seconds, until they are lightly golden. Remove from the oil and place on paper towels. Dust with sugar and serve while still warm.

LIVORNO
1915-21

INDEXES

Contents divided by Markets

Analytical index

BEANS

BEEF

BREAD

CHEESE

CHESTNUT

CHICKEN

CHOCOLATE

FISH

HONEY

LARDO

MIXED MEATS

MUSHROOM

ONION

PANCETTA

PASTA

PEARS

POLENTA

PORK

POTATO

RICE

SAUSAGE

SUGAR

TOMATOES

TUNA

VEGETABLES

ZUCCHINI

Acknowledgments

I would like to thank my family—my mom Anna and my dad Felice, Claudia and grandma Marcella—for their unwavering support as I followed my dreams and satisfied my curiosity, and for always making me feel at home in the place we all come together most naturally, the kitchen. You are my strength and my safe harbor.

Thank you, Tommaso, for being at my side through every stage of writing this book: from the moment the idea was born as we walked along the Arno River in Florence, to our trips around Tuscany in search of markets, photographs, recipes and interesting producers, and finally the days spent writing and testing recipes. I could never have done this without you, and this book is as much yours as it is mine—it is ours.
Thanks to our four-legged family, Noa and Wolfi, for the cuddles.

Thank you to Regula Ysewijn, Sarka Babicka, and Rossella Venezia for the chats, the constant support, the inspiration and the precious opportunity to meet and consult. Thank you Laura, Valeria, Anna, Francesca, Eleonora, Sara, Martina, Claudia, Mattia for your encouragement and friendship. A special thanks goes as well to all those friends who on more than one occasion offered to taste the recipes in this book.

All my gratitude goes to those people who, out of passion and friendship, helped me discover the markets of Tuscany, by pointing out producers, stands I should not miss, traditional local products and unique stories: Gigliola and Francesca (Florence), Kirstie (Greve in Chianti), Luisa and Martina (Val d'Orcia), Laura (Siena), Andrea (Valdarno), Annalisa, Ilaria, Giovanna and Simona of Farfalle in Cammino (Lunigiana), Annarita, Alessandro and Cinzia of Renaissance Tuscany Il Ciocco Resort & Spa (Garfagnana), Molly and Emanuela (Pistoia), Maria (Montecatini), Aurelia (Prato), Serena (Versilia), Kinzica (Pisa), Marco (Volterra), Enrica and Paolo (Livorno), and Emiko (San Miniato and Argentario).

Thank you to the following people for their enthusiastic assistance in testing recipes for this book: Alessia A., Alessia M., Anna, Anna Giulia, Benedetta, Chiara M., Chiara T., Cristina, Deborah, Elena F., Elena O., Elena S., Emanuela, Enrica, Erika, Fabiana, Franco, Gaia, Gianluca, Heather, Irene, Lara, Laura, Lidia, Lorella, Lorenza, Mariagrazia, Marica, Marilù, Martina, Melissa, Michelle, Monica, Ottavia, Patrizia, Piyanut, Rosemarie, Rossella, Sara, Simonetta, Stefania, Tamara, Valentina D., Valentina P., Veruschka, Virginia and Yu Qiong.

Thank you DishesOnly and RCR for the wonderful plates, bowls and glasses that feature in many of this book's photographs.

Text: *Giulia Scarpaleggia*
Photographs: *Giulia Scarpaleggia and Tommaso Galli*
Graphic design: *Leida Federico*
Translation: *Amy Gulick*
Editing: *Valeria Cecilia Barbon*
Production manager: *Anita Ravasio*

ISBN: 978 88 6753 441 8
Printed in the EU